THE PRINCETON REVIEW

TRASHPROOF RESUMES

Books in The Princeton Review Series

Cracking the ACT
Cracking the ACT with Sample Tests on Computer Disk
Cracking the GED
Cracking the GMAT
Cracking the GMAT with Sample Tests on Computer Disk
Cracking the GRE
Cracking the GRE with Sample Tests on Computer Disk
Cracking the GRE Psychology Subject Test
Cracking the LSAT
Cracking the LSAT with Sample Tests on Computer Disk
Cracking the MCAT
Cracking the MCAT with Sample Tests on Computer Disk
Cracking the SAT and PSAT
Cracking the SAT and PSAT with Sample Tests on Computer Disk
Cracking the SAT II: Biology Subject Test
Cracking the SAT II: Chemistry Subject Test
Cracking the SAT II: English Subject Tests
Cracking the SAT II: French Subject Test
Cracking the SAT II: History Subject Tests
Cracking the SAT II: Math Subject Tests
Cracking the SAT II: Physics Subject Test
Cracking the SAT II: Spanish Subject Test
Cracking the TOEFL with Audiocassette

Culturescope
Culturescope Elementary
Culturescope High School

SAT Math Workout
SAT Verbal Workout

Don't Be a Chump!
How to Survive Without Your Parents' Money
Speak Now
Trashproof Resumes

Grammar Smart
Math Smart
Reading Smart
Study Smart
Word Smart: Building an Educated Vocabulary
Word Smart II: How to Build a More Educated Vocabulary
Word Smart Executive
Word Smart Genius
Writing Smart

Grammar Smart Junior
Math Smart Junior
Word Smart Junior
Writing Smart Junior

Law School Companion

Student Access Guide to America's Top Internships
Student Access Guide to College Admissions
Student Access Guide to the Best Business Schools
Student Access Guide to the Best Law Schools
Student Access Guide to the Best Medical Schools
Student Access Guide to the Best 309 Colleges
Student Access Guide to Paying for College
Student Access Guide to Visiting College Campuses
Student Access Guide: The Big Book of Colleges
Student Access Guide: The Internship Bible

Also available on cassette from Living Language

Grammar Smart
Word Smart
Word Smart II

THE PRINCETON REVIEW

TRASHPROOF RESUMES

YOUR GUIDE TO CRACKING THE JOB MARKET

BY TIMOTHY D. HAFT

Random House, Inc.
New York 1995

Copyright © 1995 by Princeton Review Publishing, L.L.C.

All rights reserved under International and Pan-American Copyright Conventions. Published in the United States by Random House, Inc., New York, and simultaneously in Canada by Random House of Canada Limited, Toronto.

Library of Congress Cataloging-in-Publication Data

Haft, Timothy D.
Trashproof Resumes / by Timothy D. Haft.—1st ed.
p. cm.
At head of title: The Princeton Review.
ISBN 0-679-75911-5
1. Resumes (Employment) 2. College graduates—Employment.
I. Princeton Review (Firm) II. Title.
HF5383.H17 1995
808'.06665—dc20

95-6411
CIP

ISBN 0-679-75911-5

Manufactured in the United States of America on recycled paper

9 8 7 6 5 4 3 2

DEDICATION

For Brent and Margaux

It's infinitely more important to do good in real life
than it is to look good on paper.

Acknowledgments

Thanks to everyone who helped to make this dream become a reality. Special thanks to the entire Princeton Review team; to Cynthia Brantley for her patient guidance; to Susan Cohen and Chris Kensler for their editorial help; to Michelle Dicicco for her wonderful illustrations; to Maureen McMahon for believing in this book; to Jean Krier for getting the word out; to Trudy Steinfeld and the entire staff at the New York University Office of Career Services; to mom and dad for all their love and support; to Grandma Mabel for teaching me to never quit; to Lis and Jim for their unceasing encouragement; to Sandy for his unrivaled generosity and friendship; and to Suzanne, for showing me how to laugh, and for trying to teach me how to be funny.

CONTENTS

FOREWORD

In 1981 I was a naive fourth-year history major at the University of Virginia, getting ready to leave the cocoon of academia and make my mark on the world. I wasn't sure what I wanted to do with my life, but I knew I had to start paying back my student loans. So, I began to look for a job. My first stop was the university's Office of Career Planning and Placement, where a friendly counselor tried his best to help me. Unfortunately, by the time I saw him I was so mixed up that a team of twenty psychologists would have thrown their hands up and walked away.

But there was one thing I was certain about. I needed a resume and I needed it fast. "No problem," I thought to myself. I dug up my dad's trusty old manual typewriter and a fresh piece of onion skin paper, and got down to work. I was proud of the end result. Only a few minor smudges around the edges and one or two mistakes I could easily correct with white-out.

Did You Know . . .

If all the resumes currently in circulation were laid out end to end, they would circle the earth fifteen times.

Source: Professional Association of Resume Writers

In retrospect my first resume wasn't bad at all—it was awful! It violated every rule of resume writing ever known to mankind. Looking back, I can't believe anyone seriously considered me for a job after seeing that resume. In fact, I ended up in jail because of that resume—my first job out of college was at Riker's Island. A pretty harsh sentence for a bad resume.

Six years after my inauspicious resume-writing debut I became a career counselor at New York University's Office of Career Services, teaching resume writing. Since 1988 I have critiqued, edited, and written over five thousand resumes and taught over fifty resume-writing workshops. Although I have never seen a resume as bad as my own first attempt, I've gleaned that most people find resume writing an extremely difficult process. Mention the word "resume," and they get that angst-ridden, twisted look on their face like the figure in Edvard Munch's *The Scream*. Even some of the most brilliant people I've ever met can't seem to get the knack of putting their life's accomplishments on paper.

The problem is that few of us are given the slightest bit of instruction on how to write a resume before we reach college. We get a healthy dose of gym, shop, and finger painting, but no resume writing. In college, we may have the opportunity to take a resume-writing workshop or meet a few times with a career counselor. That's hardly enough to learn how to effectively put your life on a page. *Trashproof Resumes* is designed to tell you everything you ever wanted to know about resumes but didn't have the chance to ask. Think of us as your resume coach whose goal is to help you create a trashproof resume—one that stays out of waste baskets and helps you *get job interviews*. A great resume offers other benefits too by helping you secure employment, getting your parents and creditors off your back about your finances, providing insight on the kind of work you'd like to pursue, reducing your career anxiety, and building your self-confidence by illuminating the many skills and talents you possess.

WHO THIS BOOK IS FOR

This book is geared toward college students and recent college graduates (although the principles behind writing a resume are the same for college seniors, senior vice presidents, and senior citizens alike). The information in these pages is designed to address the kinds of questions that students often ask about their resumes on topics such as grades, transfer credits, study abroad, internships, lack of relevant professional experience, and describing extracurricular activities. The sample resumes throughout the book are based on those of actual college students and recent graduates seeking positions in a wide variety of fields: the commercial and performing arts, business, engineering, health care, non-profit management, social service, wildlife management, and many others.

HOW TO USE *TRASHPROOF RESUMES*

Trashproof Resumes is a workbook which is best read sequentially, since the chapters build on one another. Do not turn directly to the sample resumes! We recognize that doing so is a strong temptation, akin to devouring the chocolate mousse before you've eaten your main course, but it is a temptation worth resisting. The samples will be much more helpful after you've read the remainder of the book.

A number of exercises appear throughout the book. They are designed to help, not torment, you. They are not especially time consuming, and are well worth your effort. You'll find that by committing your thoughts and feelings to paper, they often become more lucid, refined, and meaningful.

You will also find interspersed throughout the book numerous tips, tricks, and suggestions contributed by a variety of employment experts from all around the country. Keep in mind that these are merely opinions for you to consider. A resume is a highly subjective document, and the final decision on how to prepare it is yours.

Best of luck with your job search!

Timothy D. Haft

September 1994

INTRODUCTION

WHY DO YOU NEED A RESUME?

Because you need a job. To get a job you need an interview, and to get an interview you almost always need a resume. If you have connections in high places, you probably don't need a resume—or this book. The rest of us write resumes because employers have decided that reviewing personal qualifications on a piece of paper is the most efficient way to screen job applicants. No employer has the time to meet or speak individually with every person who applies for a job. No employer has the time to read your autobiography. You need a resume because those with the power to hire you for a job say so.

THE LIMITATIONS OF A RESUME

A well-written, precisely tailored resume can help you obtain job interviews. During the interview the resume can guide the interviewer directly to your professional strengths, particularly those that relate most closely to the position for which you are applying. After the interview, your resume remains to remind employers of your key qualifications. But the buck stops there. No resume, however outstanding, gets a job offer. You do. A resume does not speak for you, dress you suitably, shake hands firmly for you, or teach you body language techniques. Looking great on paper is important, but it mostly serves to set the tone for the main act—the interview. As they say in hockey, you must be able to finish. Just as a perfect setup is wasted if you don't score, a trashproof resume is for nought if you don't succeed at the interview.

SELLING YOURSELF

In crude economics you are a product, the resume is your advertisement, and the employer is the consumer. Or, if you are a recently released film, your resume is a "coming attraction," and the employer is the moviegoer. We think you get the picture. Your goal is to convince the employer that you are worth considering for a job. Your resume is one of the best ways you have to do this. It must entice, intrigue, and prove to the employer that you have the ability to get the job done. It must distinguish you from the competition. Your resume must sell you!

BE CONCEITED

Because the competition is so stiff, you've got to toot your own horn. If you don't tell the employer about your skills and talents, who will? No one is going to whisper in her ear about how wonderful you are. That is *your* job. Of course, you must be careful not to get carried away. After all, you are not exactly a Pepsi, BMW, or a pair of Calvin Klein underwear. The fairly lax rules of advertising that apply to these products don't apply to human beings. Be reasonably honest. Make sure that the information on your resume is accurate. Even a small lie, if detected, could put a quick end to your job candidacy.

REALITY BITES

It is not unusual for an employer to receive over two hundred resumes for a single job vacancy. This allows employers to be extremely selective about granting interviews. Because the job market is an employers' market, you must write your resume with their needs in mind.

First and foremost you must communicate to the employer that you have the skills and qualifications they need. Think of yourself as a problem solver. Their problem may be selling 3D glasses, providing a shuttle service to the airport, building condominiums on Mars, or revitalizing the president's image. Whatever the employer's need, your resume must convince him that you can help him fulfill that need.

Resume Games

Several employment recruiters, citing the unmanageable number of resumes they receive, have confessed to some unorthodox screening practices. One recruiter admitted to reading only every tenth resume. Another described a sorting ritual whereby resumes were flung at a wastebasket, and only those not landing in the trash were read. Yet another recruiter recounted his department's practice of tossing resumes down the stairs—those that landed on the even steps were reviewed, the others were pitched. The moral: you may need to send several resumes to certain companies to ensure that one gets read.

Source: Professional Association of Resume Writers

PLAYING DETECTIVE

The tricky part, of course, is figuring out what the employer's needs are. If you are applying for an advertised position, the employer's needs most likely are stated in the ad. However, since many jobs are never advertised, you will not always have this luxury. It will be up to you to play detective and figure out what qualifications the employer is seeking. The information you need can be gathered from the following sources.

THE PROSPECTIVE EMPLOYER

The best place to start is the source itself. Call your prospective employer's public affairs, public relations, or human resources department. Let the person on the phone know that you are investigating employment opportunities with her firm. Ask her to send any available information—annual reports, brochures, newsletters, etc. Offer to pick up the materials in person if she is reluctant to mail them.

Researching Your Target Organization

According to Dorothy London, career libarian at Columbia University's Office of Career Services, researching an organization properly requires approaching your subject from a variety of angles. It's not enough to just read the information provided by the company itself. You also have to obtain current information from newspapers such as *The Wall Street Journal* and from business magazines and directories like those published by Dun & Bradstreet and Standard & Poors. You should even pay a visit to the site of your potential employer to get a first-hand look at the people who work there.

THE CAREER PLANNING CENTER

If you are affiliated with a college or university, ask the career planning office for information on your prospective employer. Organizations that recruit on campus often send a substantial information package prior to their recruitment visit. These packages are especially helpful because in addition to standard promotional materials, they sometimes contain detailed descriptions of the various jobs available within the organization. Also find out if your career planning office maintains a list of alumni working in your field of interest. Some of them may even work at your target company and would probably be happy to sit down and chat with you.

If you have graduated school and no longer live near your alma mater, find out if your college's career planning office has a reciprocity agreement with a college near you. You may be able to use some of the career resources at that college.

THE PUBLIC LIBRARY

A reference librarian can be a goldmine of information. Explain to him that you're in the process of a job search and would like to find out where you can learn more about prospective employers. You may be directed to several sources, including directories, trade publications, books, and annual reports. Many libraries also have computerized databases and information services which allow you to search on-line for magazine and newspaper articles about organizations you are targeting in your job search.

THE INSIDERS

Insiders who work at your targeted organizations or their competitors are often the best sources of information. They have the "inside scoop" and can provide you with classified knowledge that would be impossible to obtain anywhere else. Unfortunately, it is not always easy to find an informant. You may not have an Uncle Joe or Aunt Sue who works in your targeted industry. Your best bet is to check with your university's career planning or alumni relations office to see if they can provide you with a list of alumni working in your field of interest.

PRIORITIZE

In large part, the way you prepare your resume will be dictated by what you've learned about your potential employer. You'll need to prioritize your qualifications so they mesh with the employer's needs. Start with your most impressive credentials. If you're applying for a job on Wall Street and have outstanding business experience, lead off your resume with your experience section. If you're seeking a job as a computer programmer and have expertise in every programming language ever devised, start the resume with your computer skills section.

By emphasizing your relevant strengths early in the resume, there is a good chance you will make a strong positive impression on the reader right off the bat. That's important because many employers skim resumes rather quickly, and if nothing piques their curiosity right away, they may not bother reading the rest.

DON'T WORRY, BE HAPPY

If using a skill makes you miserable, there is no sense stressing it on your resume—no matter how much it may increase your marketability. Keep in mind that by emphasizing a skill on your resume, you will be expected to talk about that skill at length during the interview. If hired, you will be expected to demonstrate that skill and put it to good use. So unless you are absolutely desperate for a job, highlighting an ability that you would rather keep in the closet is generally not wise.

Imagine that your dream is to write for *Spin* magazine. Also imagine that you type one hundred words a minute and that you enjoy typing about as much as you enjoy studying for finals. On the one hand, stressing your exceptional typing speed on your resume may encourage someone at *Spin* to give you a second look. On the other hand, your exceptional typing speed will probably relegate you to the ranks of the typing pool, destined to spend long hours at the keyboard every day. "That's okay," you say to yourself, "I've got my foot in the door, and eventually I will prove myself to be the great writer I know I am." The question is, how long can you stand typing before you pick up your IBM Selectric and smash it over your boss' head? What toll will all the dreaded typing take on your mind, body, and spirit? Do typists at *Spin* have the slimmest chance of being promoted? Only you can answer these questions, but in general, if you want to be a writer, then look for a job which will allow you to write, not just type.

Career Fair Heaven

If you're a career fair maniac, the College Placement Council publishes a list of over 1,700 career days and job fairs indexed geographically. Although the publication is mostly used by career counselors, you can get your own copy by calling (800) 544-5272. Just remember that many career fairs are off-limits to students and alumni who do not attend the sponsoring school.

Popcorn, Peanuts, Pretzels, Anyone?

The number of college graduates working as street vendors increased from 57,000 in 1983 to 75,000 in 1990.

Source: Bureau of Labor Statistics

CUSTOMIZING YOUR RESUME

If you are job hunting in more than one field, or considering different types of positions within a field, you will need to have more than one version of your resume. For example, let's assume you are applying for two jobs: an account representative at an advertising agency and an editorial assistant at a publishing house. For each position you need to stress different skills on your resume. For the account rep job you need to emphasize your interpersonal, communication, sales, and marketing skills. For the editorial assistant slot you need to stress your attention to detail, ability to work under deadline pressure, and skills as a proofreader and editor. Naturally, there will be some overlap on the resumes, but the thrust of each should be very different.

The Toughest Part About Writing a Resume Is . . .

"Making myself appear as exalted on paper as I really am in person."

—Anu Ailawadhi, public relations professional, graduate of Marist College

"Demonstrating my best qualities without coming off like I'm bragging."

—Julia Sergeyev, Director of Production, Digital Color Edge

"Deciding where to begin, since the process can be so overwhelming."

—Bruce Arbit, Development Associate, Jacob Riis Neighborhood Settlement House

"Conveying what you did and the manner in which you did it."

—Lucy Hol, intern, Avon, and senior, New York University's Stern School of Business

"Writing a coherent summary statement or objective."

—Diann Witt, graduate, University of Nebraska

OVERCOMING RESUMEPHOBIA

Most people *hate* writing resumes. They view the task as a necessary evil, like doing the laundry or taking out the garbage. Many people are also *afraid* of writing their resumes, and either avoid the process altogether or hire people to write their resumes for them. Avoidance leaves you without a resume and clearly limits the scope of your job search. Hiring a pro to write your resume may reduce your anxiety level, but excludes the experience of writing your own resume, the best tune-up of all for job interviews. Besides, wouldn't you rather spend your hard-earned money on a vacation to Europe, a new pair of rollerblades, or some extra long bungee cords?

WHY PEOPLE HATE AND FEAR RESUMES

There are five main reasons for humankind's hatred and fear of writing resumes. It is important to elaborate on these, because if you can understand your hatred and fear of resumes, you can conquer any debilitating feelings you may have toward them.

I THINK, THEREFORE I AM MY RESUME

Many people have the sense that their total worth is summed up by their resume. Don't feel this way. People are for the most part thinking, feeling, caring beings with souls. A resume is a piece of paper covered with black ink. You are not the sum of your resume any more than you are equal to your GPA or GRE score. Resumes, grades, and test scores are simply modern conveniences designed to make screening, sorting, and categorizing individuals easier.

ANXIETY

Creating a resume implies that you are looking for a job. Looking for a job means potential change, and change causes stress and anxiety. The change could be leaving McDonald's for Burger King, or it could be graduating from college and searching for your first professional job. In either case, an outlet is needed for anxiety. The scapegoat is frequently the poor resume. It gets yelled at, crumpled into a ball, thrown across the room, ripped to shreds, burned, stomped, and tossed in the microwave. But of course the resume isn't to blame. People are simply afraid of what it represents. With great trepidation, people ask themselves: Am I marketable? What will employers think of my credentials? Will my job hunt be successful? Will I be able to pay the rent? The hell with the rent, what about food? And so on.

This type of anxiety is perfectly normal, but it needs to be placed in proper perspective. In general, everyone tends to exaggerate the potential downside of an unsuccessful job search. What is the worst thing that could possibly happen? So what if you impose on your friends or relatives for a while until something turns up? They'll forgive you. The main thing is to believe in yourself, and to be confident that no matter what, everything is going to work out fine. And it will.

The Five Most Effective Stress-Busters
1. Shiatsu massage
2. moshing
3. yoga
4. flotation tank
5. synchroenergizer

My Life Is Bigger Than That

The anxious resumephobe, in a typical fit, screams, "How can I put my whole life story on one page? I have done so many amazing things that I need at least five pages to do my accomplishments justice." Wrong. A resume is not your autobiography. It is a summary of your qualifications . . . a highlight reel. Employers do not need or want all the gory details. On a resume, as in life, less is often more.

My Life Is Zippo

The deflated resumephobe sighs, "I haven't done anything in my life. I'll never be able to fill up one page." Wrong. If you think you haven't accomplished anything in life, the odds are you don't know yourself very well. Ask your friends and family members to give their opinions of your skills and strengths. Everyone has a unique combination of skills, accomplishments, and experiences that makes him special. Everyone is different, and almost everyone, regardless of how checkered her work history may be, has something positive to offer an employer. Besides, as you will see later, a resume is much more than a collection of job descriptions.

I Can't Write

You claim you don't write very well? Good. Skilled writers often have a great deal of difficulty writing good resumes. Resumes are concise, factual documents. They are not places for elegant prose or exquisite style. Simple, direct language will do just fine. You don't even have to follow all the rules of grammar. If you can write a simple sentence, you can write a great resume.

CHAPTER 1

SELF ASSESSMENT

WHAT DO YOU WANT TO DO WITH YOUR LIFE?

Ironically, the most dreaded question you'll ever have to face during the course of your college years will not be asked in the classroom. Instead, it will be asked while you are home during Spring Break of your senior year. Your mother or father will come up to you with that anxious look and then before you have a chance to bolt, they'll pop the question: "So what are you going to do after graduation?" Your silence will be deafening, as will their yelling and screaming about how much they shelled out for your education, and that they better get a good return on their investment. And, as if that isn't bad enough, before you know it everyone else will jump on the bandwagon. Aunts, uncles, grandparents, distant cousins, neighbors, and even local shopkeepers will ask what you'll be doing after graduation. It's no wonder so many recent graduates want to relocate thousands of miles from home.

The Best Cities for New College Graduates (from *Managing Your Career*, the college edition of the *National Business Employment Weekly*, Spring 1994, published by *The Wall Street Journal*)

Note that large markets have more than 500,000 jobs in their economy, medium markets have between 150,000 and 500,000, and small markets have fewer than 150,000 jobs.

Large Markets

1. Salt Lake City, UT
2. Indianapolis, IN
3. Nashville, TN
4. Louisville, KY
5. Greensboro/Winston-Salem, NC

Medium Markets

1. Madison, WI
2. Austin, TX
3. Lake County, IL
4. Raleigh/Durham, NC
5. Omaha, NE

Small Markets

1. Sioux Falls, SD
2. Provo, UT
3. Boise, ID
4. Santa Fe, NM
5. Rapid City, SD

Be Yourself

"To be nobody but yourself in a world which is doing its best, night and day, to make you everybody else means to fight the hardest battle which any human being can fight, and never stop fighting."

— e.e. cummings

Whether you are still in school or have already been around the block a few times, figuring out what you want to do for a living is no easy task. There are tremendous pressures, both internal and external, to make a quick decision. A common tendency among students and recent grads is to jump right into the job hunt and accept the first offer that comes along. This can be a huge mistake, and is often the start of a vicious cycle of drifting aimlessly from job to job.

So why is this issue being raised in a book on resumes? Because, dear reader, until you figure out where you're heading with your career, writing an effective resume will be next to impossible. It would be like creating an advertisement for an unknown product that will be marketed to an unknown audience. How can you decide what skills to stress on your resume if you're not sure what you want to do? And how can you address the needs of a prospective employer if you don't even know the field in which you want to work? Now don't get us wrong. We're not saying you won't be able to find a job just because you don't know what you'd like to do for a living. Of course you'll be able to find a job, but the odds are overwhelmingly in favor of it being the wrong job.

It's kind of like those muffler commercials . . . you can pay now, or you can pay later. It makes more sense to do some serious self-assessment now and figure out what you really want to do than to jump at the first job that comes along. Better that you bag groceries, scoop ice cream, or walk dogs until you sort things out. Those of you who are one hundred percent sure about what you want in a career are truly fortunate. The rest of you, don't worry. A careful reading of this chapter and a few years of psychotherapy and the answer will come.

THE THREE BUILDING BLOCKS OF CAREER PLANNING

As one of our former students put it, "how the #$%* do you figure out what you want to do with your life?" There are no magic answers. However, as with all mysteries, there are some good clues. For the most part, these clues fall into three categories: interests, skills, and values. If you can figure out what you are passionate about, where your talents lie, and what you want from work, then you are well on the way to finding your true calling.

INTERESTS

Imagine how it would feel to actually enjoy earning your livelihood. What a great feeling to wake up in the morning and look forward to the challenges that lie ahead in the workplace. What a rush to be so engrossed in your work that you don't even notice the passing of the day. When your work is interesting, you feel fulfilled, energized, focused, and yes, even happy.

On the flip side, if your work is dull, routine, insignificant, and boring, the negative consequences are enormous. You start to shrivel up inside. You lose your energy, spark, motivation, and even some of your brain cells. Inevitably you burn out on your job and either quit, get fired, become a vegetable, or terrorize your co-workers with automatic weapons.

Figuring out your interests is worthwhile and simple. The following exercises give you a good start.

YOUR FAVORITE ACTIVITIES

Take a few minutes to fill in the following blanks. List the ten activities that you enjoy most. It is not important if they appear to be unrelated. Indicate how often (daily, weekly, monthly) you engage in these activities. You may be surprised to find out that you have been neglecting what makes you happiest.

Now look at your list carefully and place a star next to any activity that could be performed in a work-related setting. For example, if shopping made your top ten, think about the work that one might do as a buyer or personal shopper. Believe it or not, just about everything you want to do for fun can be connected with work. You can throw the adage "Don't mix business with pleasure" right out the window. Try to generate ten occupational options based on your list. Get a counselor, friend, or someone who knows you well to help. You'll be surprised how many realistic career options will emerge from a couple of good brainstorming sessions.

The Long Haul

It's one thing to get stuck in a job for a few months, but imagine staying in the same field for 98 years. According to the Guiness Book of World Records, Mr. Izumi began working at a sugar mill in Japan in 1872 and retired as a sugar cane farmer in 1970 at the robust age of 105.

Follow Your Dreams

"What I finally realized . . . was, frankly, that I didn't enjoy what I was doing. There are probably a lot of people out there like me who end up doing something, and they get caught up in a career. What happens is you find yourself twenty years later down the road and . . . you say, why? Take some time off, whether you want to go to Europe for half a year or to California and get a job as a bartender for a year, or Florida and work on the beach at Ft. Lauderdale . . . . The primary reason is not only to have some fun while you're young and healthy, but to really think through your career before you start. Try to keep your options open. Because whoever you work for will be keeping their options open. If you have an itch, scratch it. If you have an urge, pursue it. If you have a dream, try to follow it."

—Gary Wilber, former CEO,
Drug Emporium, Inc.
Source: *The Wall Street Journal*

Favorite Activities	Frequency of Participation
1. _____	_____
2. _____	_____
3. _____	_____
4. _____	_____
5. _____	_____
6. _____	_____
7. _____	_____
8. _____	_____
9. _____	_____
10. _____	_____

Occupational Options Based on Your Favorite Activities

1. _____
2. _____
3. _____
4. _____
5. _____
6. _____
7. _____
8. _____
9. _____
10. _____

WINNING THE LOTTERY

Imagine winning the Publishers Clearinghouse Sweepstakes. Your money worries are over. The only financial decision you have to make is whether you want your money in $250,000 quarterly installments or $1,000,000 at the beginning of each year. Let's also assume that you have all the education necessary to pursue any career. You can do whatever you want with your winnings provided that you continue to work. No eternal shopping sprees or permanent vacations allowed.

Now find a quiet, peaceful place, a sanctuary where you can contemplate your future without being disturbed. Put on some Enya or Kitaro—any New Age music will do. Let your imagination run wild, unencumbered by practical considerations. Remember, money and education are no longer obstacles. What kind of work would you do? Try to describe how you would spend your time. What would your physical work environment look like? Do you see yourself outdoors, behind a desk, or in a space station? Who would you be interacting with—corporate executives, migrant workers, college students? How would you dress? In a suit and tie, Gap attire, or grunge? What would a typical day be like? In what types of activities would you be engaged? Would you be analyzing the rise in interest rates, reporting on Madonna's latest affair, finding new homes for foster children, selling hi-technology, researching DNA and its link with disease? Try to conjure up as vivid an image of your work day as possible. Write down every detail you can remember. If at first you have difficulty with this exercise, don't worry. Give it a rest and try again when you are feeling more relaxed.

OCCUPATIONAL FANTASIES

Have you ever fantasized about what you would like to do for a living? Do you have the same aspirations you had when you were a child? Make a list of all the occupational fantasies you've had over the course of your life. For each, indicate your age at the time, and what factors you believe led to the origination of the fantasy. Have your dreams and fantasies changed over time? Do you notice any patterns or trends?

Childhood _____

_____

_____

Adolescence _____

_____

_____

Adulthood _____

_____

_____

INTEREST INVENTORIES

Discuss with a career counselor the possibility of taking an interest inventory such as the Strong Interest Inventory or the Campbell Interest and Skills Survey. Both inventories are available at many college career planning centers, or through private career consultants. Interest inventories are not tests—there are no right and wrong answers. It is impossible to fail. What the inventories attempt to do is measure your level of interest in several basic areas (math, science, art, teaching, sales, law, and so on) and compare your pattern of likes and dislikes to those of professionals in a wide variety of occupations. The premise of interest inventories is that birds of a feather flock together. Thus, the more similar your interests are to the interests of a certain occupational group, the more likely you are to be comfortable within that group.

One thing interest inventories do not indicate is whether you have the talent or training necessary to pursue a given field. For example, if your interests are identical to those of fine artists, but you have trouble drawing a stick figure, it may not a wise idea to pursue a career as a painter. Interest inventories do not provide any magic answers. They only provide information which, interpreted by a skilled practitioner, can assist you in figuring out what the #$%* you want to do.

Skills

Most college students and recent grads are incredibly modest about their abilities. During the course of a typical career counseling session, a client often remarks, "I really don't have any skills," or "I don't think I have much to offer an employer." This simply isn't true.

Let's get one thing straight—college graduates are among the elite of our nation. According to the National Center for Education Statistics, only about one in four Americans have earned a bachelor's degree. This education endows the average grad with dozens of marketable skills. The problem is he just doesn't know it. What does this have to do with choosing a career? Everything. If you want to enjoy your work, it is absolutely crucial that you use your talents on the job, especially those you enjoy most. These are the skills that turn you on, rev you up, and get your motor going. Possessing a skill is meaningless if you don't want to put it into practice. For example, imagine that you are a very talented computer programmer, but would rather analyze the rhythm patterns of Brazilian samba than write a program. If that's the case, you might as well stuff your programming skills into a hard drive and toss the hard drive out of a fast-moving vehicle.

Learning About Your Skills Through Your Accomplishments

So how do you figure out what skills you possess and really enjoy using? One approach is to think back over your lifetime and write down the five accomplishments of which you are most proud. They need not be work-related at all. For example, one accomplishment might be the time you backpacked your way through Iraq while wearing a "Saddam Sucks" T-shirt. Another might be that successful naked co-ed ski trip you organized.

Once you've thought of your top five accomplishments, take out a sheet of paper. Now get set to write five illuminating stories. In vivid detail try to recreate each accomplishment as carefully, precisely, and graphically as possible. When you are done, review the stories methodically, and try to extract from them the skills you utilized to do whatever it was you did. Be generous with yourself. Did you use communication skills? Organization skills? Analytical skills? Foreign language skills?

List at least ten skills for each of the five stories. Put a star next to those skills which you particularly enjoyed using. Now go over your list again. Do you notice any patterns? Are there certain skills that keep popping up on each list? If so, make a note of them. If you discover that all your accomplishments center on writing, you may want to investigate a career in journalism or publishing. If, on the other hand, most of your accomplishments focus on your interpersonal skills, you may want to explore fields such as psychology, human resources, or sales.

If you have a tough time with any portion of this exercise, get a friend, relative, or counselor to help you out. This is not an easy exercise. Nor is it short. But it's worth it.

Different Skills For Different Thrills

Let's get to work classifying your skills. Your goal is to determine where your skills lie, as well as which skills you most enjoy. Start with four broad categories: people (e.g., teaching); data and information (e.g., researching); things (e.g., assembling); and ideas (e.g., creating). You may find that the skills you most enjoy all involve dealing with people. If this is the case, you will probably want a job or career characterized by a high degree of personal contact. If you're a people person but you're in a job that requires you to crunch numbers all day, the prognosis for happiness is not good.

In addition to the people/data/things/ideas breakdown, skills can be further classified as either transferable or content-specific. Transferable skills are generic, acquired throughout life in a variety of informal and formal settings. They can usually be applied in just about any work environment. Some common transferable skills are organizing, listening, teaching, and leading.

Content-specific skills are specialized and generally acquired through formal education or on-the-job training. They consist of the of knowledge and abilities that are required to work in a particular field. Examples of content-specific skills include computer programming, financial planning, writing press releases, translating French into English, and preparing corporate tax returns. These skills are not directly transferable from one career field to another.

Creating Your Personal Skills Inventory

Review the following list of transferable skills and circle the ones in which you believe you have some proficiency. On a separate sheet of paper cite a specific example that demonstrates how you used each of the circled skills. Put a check next to those skills that you most enjoy using. Put a line through those that you loathe using. Star the skills you don't currently possess but would like to acquire. This exercise will give you a clearer picture of the responsibilities you might enjoy taking on in your next job, as well as those you might want to avoid.

People Skills

caring	listening	counseling
collaborating	advocating	motivating
managing	delegating	supervising
teaching	facilitating	training
resolving conflicts	persuading	oral communication
interviewing	coaching	guiding
advising	empathizing	

Skills With Data and Information

analyzing facts	compiling information	classifying information
working with numbers	budgeting	taking inventory
allocating resources	computing	systematizing
testing hypotheses	computer programming	using logic
record keeping	extrapolating	interpolating
summarizing	translating	editing
tabulating		

Skills With Things

manual dexterity	repairing machines	using tools
operating machines	assembling	installing
building/constructing	cooking	navigating
farming	physical coordination	lifting
handling	carrying	

Skills With Ideas

imagining	improvising	innovating
experimenting	synthesizing	designing
creating music or art	symbolizing	writing plays/poetry
visualizing	acting	inventing
conceptualizing		

Create a list of all your content-specific skills. In what areas have you developed some degree of expertise? Are you a sports nut, wine connoisseur, civil war buff, computer whiz, shutterbug, aspiring musician, motorcycle maven, or art aficionado? Any subject, no matter how trivial it may seem to you, is fair game for this list. Put a check next to the subjects you are most passionate about. Are you considering pursuing one of these areas as a career? If so, in what capacity would you want to work? Are there new skills that you need to acquire? Will you need to go back to school, or alter your current curriculum if you're already in school?

VALUES

For work to be truly fulfilling, it must satisfy some of the values that you hold dear to your heart. In a sense, your motivation to work is derived from the pursuit of these values. They give you a *raison d'être*. Are you driven by power, prestige, intellectual challenge, or helping others? Your answer plays a major role in determining your career direction. If money is most important to you, it makes sense to consider occupations that have high income potential. If it's job security you seek, it's a good idea to look into professions that have proven stable over time.

Keep in mind that almost every career or job choice involves some form of compromise. While you can't always get everything you want, if you know yourself well you can at least minimize the likelihood that your values will conflict with your career choice. If you place a high premium on creativity, for example, then it would probably not be wise to accept a highly structured position within an organization that rewards conventionality. Likewise, if one of your values is saving the environment, then working for a Styrofoam manufacturer might not be the best choice. To avoid conflicts between your personal values and your career, you need both to know yourself and to carefully research potential career fields.

What Do You Want From Your Work?

Take a good look at the following list of work-related values. Keep in mind what you honestly want from a career—not what your family or friends want, but what you want. After giving it some thought, circle the three values you consider most important. If you had to compromise, which of the three would you give up? Which could you never give up? How do your current career plans match up with the values you most cherish? What steps can you take to avoid conflict between your values and your career plans?

Work-Related Values

expertise	authority	creativity
variety	help society	supportive colleagues
autonomy	status	flexible schedule
intellectual stimulation	high income	time off
pleasant surroundings	benefits	career advancement
travel	job security	

My Three Most-Cherished Values

1. _____

2. _____

3. _____

Putting It All Together

If you've worked through this chapter thoroughly, you have a bunch of lists and ideas written down. Now take a moment to reflect on all the exercises you so diligently completed. See the big picture coming into sharper focus? What activities really hold your interest? Which skills do you most enjoy using? Which ones would you never want to use even if you got paid royally? Do you have a preference for working with people, data, things, or ideas? What are the values that you would like to satisfy through your work? What kind of rewards are you looking for? Are you Mr. Corporate America, Rafael Artiste, or Angela Non-Profit? After you come to your own conclusions, you may want to consult with the people who know you best. Hopefully these exercises have helped you gain a better sense of your interests, skills, and values, and the direction in which you want to take them.

CHAPTER 2

PUTTING YOURSELF ON PAPER

Like a sculpture in progress, your resume is an emerging work of art that must be prodded, molded, and caressed to obtain the desired result. Instead of clay, stone, or steel, the medium is words. With words you will gracefully and eloquently compose your final masterpiece. But before you can find the right words, you need information. The information required is essentially a comprehensive inventory of your own accomplishments, experiences, and skills you've attained from work, school, and life in general. You will be recording this information on the worksheets that follow, and using it later as the raw material for the rough draft of your resume.

To make your task more manageable, you may want to enlist the help of employers, co-workers, professors, friends, acquaintances, and anyone else who may recall some of your more memorable and noteworthy exploits. Certain documents such as school transcripts, old job descriptions, and letters of recommendation could also come in handy. If you have trouble recalling the details of a job, you may want to consult the *Dictionary of Occupational Titles* (located in most major libraries), which offers a concise description for just about every occupation imaginable.

In compiling your personal history inventory, be as thorough and descriptive as possible. You can always edit later on. Also, although some of the information may not end up on the final draft of your resume, it may prove helpful when you fill out a job application. Because of this, always bring a copy of your completed inventory with you on interviews. You never know when you'll be asked to submit an employment application.

Your Personal History Inventory

Graduate School Education

1. Name of institution _____

2. Location of institution (city and state) _____

3. Dates of attendance _____

4. Degree _____

5. Thesis topic and description _____

_____

_____

6. Course of study _____

7. Research interests _____

8. Overall GPA _____

9. Courses completed and grades received _____

_____

_____

10. Significant projects/papers _____

_____

_____

11. Merit-based scholarships _____

_____

12. Academic honors _____

13. Other school–based honors or awards _____

_____

College #1

1. Name of institution _____

2. Location of institution (city and state) _____

   _____

3. Dates of attendance _____

4. Degree _____

5. Major(s) _____

6. Minor _____

7. Overall GPA _____

8. Major GPA _____

9. Class rank (if known) _____

10. Courses completed and grades received _____

    _____

    _____

    _____

11. Significant projects/papers _____

    _____

    _____

    _____

12. Merit-based scholarships _____

    _____

13. Academic honors (dean's list, Phi Beta Kappa, magna cum laude, etc. _____

    _____

14. Other school-based honors or awards _____

    _____

    _____

    _____

College #2

1. Name of institution _____

2. Location of institution (city and state) _____

   _____

3. Dates of attendance _____

4. Degree _____

5. Major(s) _____

6. Minor _____

7. Overall GPA _____

8. Major GPA _____

9. Class rank (if known) _____

10. Courses completed and grades received _____

   _____

   _____

   _____

11. Significant projects/papers _____

   _____

   _____

   _____

12. Merit-based scholarships _____

   _____

13. Academic honors (dean's list, Phi Beta Kappa, magna cum laude, etc.) _____

   _____

14. Other school-based honors or awards _____

   _____

   _____

   _____

High School Education

1. Name of institution _____

2. Location of institution (city and state) _____

   _____

3. Dates of attendance _____

4. Diploma _____

5. Curriculum _____

6. Overall GPA _____

7. Class rank (if known) _____

8. Courses completed and grades received _____

   _____

   _____

   _____

9. Merit–based scholarships _____

   _____

   _____

10. Academic honors _____

    _____

    _____

11. Other school-based honors or awards _____

    _____

    _____

    _____

Informal Education

List the classes, seminars, and workshops you have attended that were not part of your formal curriculum. For example, perhaps you are taking private acting lessons, or maybe you attended several lectures and workshops at the American Psychological Association's national convention. Make sure to indicate the name of the class, the name and location of the organization that offered it, and the year you attended.

1. _____

   _____

2. _____

   _____

3. _____

   _____

4. _____

   _____

5. _____

   _____

Standardized Test Scores

SAT _____

GRE _____

MCAT _____

LSAT _____

GMAT _____

Other tests _____

_____

_____

Work Experience

Include paid and volunteer positions, as well as internships.

Work Experience #1

1. Name of employer _____

2. Employer's address _____

3. Type of business, industry, or field _____

4. Job title _____

5. Dates of employment (month and year) _____

6. Reason for leaving _____

7. Name and phone number of direct supervisor (will this person be a reference?) _____

8. What were your major accomplishments on the job? (Were you promoted? Did you receive an award or special recognition for your service? What did you initiate, create, design, revamp?)

   _____

   _____

   _____

   _____

   _____

9. What were your major job responsibilities? In what types of tasks or activities were you typically engaged? Try to recall and record what seem like even the most mundane and obvious responsibilities.

   _____

   _____

   _____

   _____

   _____

10. What new knowledge or insights did you gain? Did you learn the ins and outs of how casting agencies operate or what makes Wall Street tick? This question is especially relevant for those who you have served as interns or volunteers. While working in a non-paid capacity it is quite common that one's responsibilities are rather menial and that the real value of the position is derived from being exposed to a field from the inside.

_____

_____

_____

_____

_____

_____

11. What skills did you acquire or improve upon? (e.g., did you become adept at public speaking?)

_____

_____

_____

_____

_____

Work Experience #2

1. Name of employer _____

2. Employer's address _____

3. Type of business, industry, or field _____

4. Job title _____

5. Dates of employment (month and year)_____

6. Reason for leaving_____

7. Name and phone number of direct supervisor (will this person be a reference?) _____

8. What were your major accomplishments on the job? _____

   _____

   _____

   _____

9. What were your major job responsibilities? _____

   _____

   _____

   _____

10. What new knowledge or insights did you gain? _____

    _____

    _____

    _____

11. What skills did you acquire or improve upon?_____

    _____

    _____

    _____

Work Experience #3

1. Name of employer _____

2. Employer's address _____

3. Type of business, industry, or field _____

4. Job title _____

5. Dates of employment (month and year)_____

6. Reason for leaving_____

7. Name and phone number of direct supervisor (will this person be a reference?) _____

8. What were your major accomplishments on the job? _____

    _____

    _____

    _____

9. What were your major job responsibilities? _____

    _____

    _____

    _____

10. What new knowledge or insights did you gain? _____

    _____

    _____

    _____

11. What skills did you acquire or improve upon?_____

    _____

    _____

    _____

Worek Experience #4

1. Name of employer _____

2. Employer's address _____

3. Type of business, industry, or field _____

4. Job title _____

5. Dates of employment (month and year)_____

6. Reason for leaving_____

7. Name and phone number of direct supervisor (will this person be a reference?) _____

8. What were your major accomplishments on the job? _____

   _____

   _____

   _____

9. What were your major job responsibilities? _____

   _____

   _____

   _____

10. What new knowledge or insights did you gain? _____

    _____

    _____

    _____

11. What skills did you acquire or improve upon?_____

    _____

    _____

    _____

Activities

List your participation in both school and extracurricular activities, such as student government, clubs and organizations (academic, career-related, social, religious, political or service), fraternities and sororities, sports, publications, and hobbies (e.g., photography, guitar playing, and so on).

Activity #1

1. Name of club, organization, or hobby _____

2. Your position or title (e.g., member, treasurer)   Were you elected to the position? _____

3. Dates of involvement _____

4. Principal activities of the club or organization_____
_____

5. What did you accomplish while involved with this activity?_____
_____
_____
_____
_____

6. What were your major responsibilities as a member of this group?
_____
_____
_____
_____

7. What skills did you acquire or improve upon?_____
_____
_____
_____
_____

Activity #2

1. Name of club, organization, or hobby _____

2. Your position or title (e.g., member, treasurer) Were you elected to the position? _____

3. Dates of involvement _____

4. Principal activities of the club or organization _____

   _____

   _____

   _____

   _____

5. What did you accomplish while involved with this activity? _____

   _____

   _____

   _____

   _____

6. What were your major responsibilities as a member of this group?

   _____

   _____

   _____

   _____

7. What skills did you acquire or improve upon? _____

   _____

   _____

   _____

   _____

Activity #3

1. Name of club, organization, or hobby _____

2. Your position or title (e.g., member, treasurer) Were you elected
   to the position? _____

3. Dates of involvement _____

4. Principal activities of the club or organization _____

   _____

   _____

   _____

   _____

5. What did you accomplish while involved with this activity? _____

   _____

   _____

   _____

   _____

6. What were your major responsibilities as a member of this group?

   _____

   _____

   _____

7. What skills did you acquire or improve upon? _____

   _____

   _____

   _____

   _____

Activity #4

1. Name of club, organization, or hobby _____

2. Your position or title (e.g., member, treasurer) Were you elected to the position? _____

3. Dates of involvement _____

4. Principal activities of the club or organization _____

   _____

   _____

   _____

   _____

5. What did you accomplish while involved with this activity? _____

   _____

   _____

   _____

   _____

6. What were your major responsibilities as a member of this group?

   _____

   _____

   _____

   _____

7. What skills did you acquire or improve upon? _____

   _____

   _____

   _____

   _____

Skills

This list should be comprised mainly of your technical or "hard" skills. "Soft" skills such as communicating, organizing, managing, and the like should be omitted from this section. For each of the skills you list, try to qualify your level of competency (beginning, intermediate, advanced). The categories below are by no means exhaustive, but they're a good place to start.

1. **Computers**—software packages, hardware, and programming languages

   _____

   _____

   _____

2. **Foreign languages**—specify whether and with what degree of proficiency you have the ability to write, read, speak, interpret, or translate

   _____

   _____

   _____

3. **Math and science**—statistics, research methodology, lab procedures

   _____

   _____

   _____

4. **Business**—cost accounting, financial analysis, economic forecasting

   _____

   _____

   _____

5. **Arts**—film editing, camera operation, set design, graphic design

   _____

   _____

   _____

References

List the names, titles, addresses, and phone numbers of at least three references.

Reference #1

Name _____

Title _____

Address _____

Phone number _____

Reference #2

Name _____

Title _____

Address _____

Phone number _____

Reference #3

Name _____

Title _____

Address _____

Phone number _____

Reference #4

Name _____

Title _____

Address _____

Phone number _____

It's a Wrap

You now have all the raw material necessary for the first draft of your resume, as well as a few chapters of your autobiography. Put your Personal History Inventory aside for now. We'll be coming back to it in chapter 6. First, you're going to learn how to choose a resume format.

CHAPTER 3

A QUESTION OF FORMAT

Choosing a resume format is a little like choosing an outfit for a night on the town. Once you've made your choice, it will limit your options for the evening's activities, and will also influence the way others perceive you. The resume format you select will dictate the organization of your qualifications on the printed page, and thus has major implications for how the reader will perceive your credentials. Two formats have predominated recent history: "reverse-chronological" and "skills based." The reverse-chronological approach has been the more popular of the two for many years, for good reason—most employers find it easier to read, and most job seekers find it easier to prepare. Nevertheless, the skills-based approach also has its proponents, and in certain situations is equally appropriate. Let's take a closer look at these two resume styles so you can determine which would be best for your situation.

REVERSE-CHRONOLOGICAL

The logic behind the reverse-chronological resume format is that professional and academic progress occur in a linear fashion. In the reverse-chronological format, the applicant's work experience and education are listed and described in sequence from most recent to least recent. This approach provides the reader with a clear sense of the applicant's career and academic progression through time. It also enables the employer to determine from a quick glance where and when the applicant worked, as well as what they accomplished at each job.

The reverse-chronological format is a good choice for job hunters whose most recent work and educational experience is closely related to their current job objective. It also favors those who have demonstrated a stable work history with few or no employment gaps. Finally, it works well for those whose careers have progressed logically toward their current objective.

The reverse-chronological format was an excellent choice for Anne Sein (see resume on page 42), who is pursuing a career in nursing. Anne chose to begin her resume with her education section, since her recent nursing degree and high grades are two of her most impressive qualifications. She then lists her work experience, which is not only directly related to her career objective, but also shows a healthy career advancement over time. This serves to reassure the employer that Anne is definitely on the right track. The reverse-chronological format is a perfect fit for her career objective. What you wouldn't know about Anne from reading this resume is that she is actually a career changer. Her previous work experience was scattered over a wide variety of fields. It was omitted because it was irrelevant. This method is not dishonest—it's an intelligent, selective marketing effort.

However, the reverse-chronological format is not for everybody. It is not for those who have an inconsistent work record, or history of job jumping. On a reverse-chronological resume, a checkered past becomes glaringly obvious. Gaps in job continuity jump off the page. The reverse-chronological approach is less effective for those whose most relevant work experiences came earlier in their career. For example, imagine that you are applying for a job as an accountant. Five years ago you worked as a bookkeeper, but since then you have been employed with the circus as a clown. On a reverse-chronological resume your experience as a clown is the first thing the employer would see. Not very promising.

Though it worked for Anne, the reverse-chronological approach may not be the best choice for career changers or those with limited experience in their chosen field. Let's say you want to get into publishing, but have no actual publishing experience. Preparing your resume in a reverse-chronological manner will only emphasize your lack of experience and give employers little cause to consider you as a serious candidate. If you find yourself in this predicament you may need to opt for the skills-based format.

REVERSE-CHRONOLOGICAL FORMAT CHECKLIST

Consider using this format if:

1. your most recent work and/or educational experience is related to your career goal
2. you have a stable work history with few or no gaps
3. your work history shows a logical progression toward your current objective
4. you want to play it safe and not risk pissing off the employer

Consider another format if:

1. you have little or no relevant work experience
2. your work history is unfocused, and you have jumped from field to field
3. you have gaping holes in your employment history

ANNE SEIN
104 Fifth Avenue
New York, NY 10028
(212) 333-3333

OBJECTIVE

Position as a staff nurse.

EDUCATION

Phillips Beth Israel School of Nursing, New York, NY
Associate in Applied Science Degree, Nursing, June 1995
Grade Point Average: 3.93

Honors:
- Dean's Honor List: all semesters
- Class Senator, 1993-1995
- Selected by faculty to participate in a conference sponsored by the Jacobs Perlow Hospice
- Representative for student body on the Faculty Curriculum Coordinating Committee

EXPERIENCE

1993-Present
Beth Israel Medical Center, New York, NY
Student Nurse Intern, Emergency Department

- Assist RNs and physicians with providing emergency care to patients in a 32-bed emergency department.
- Perform EKGs, insert foley catheters, administer glucose tests, and perform other procedures as requested under the supervision of a Registered Nurse.

1989-1992
Bud M. Weiser, M.D., New York, NY
Office Manager

- Liaison between doctor and patient.
- Coordinated hospital admissions and arranged various outpatient tests.

Handled all aspects of office management, including: insurance billing; correspondence; accounts payable and receivable; file creation and maintenance.

COMMUNITY SERVICE

- **Burden Center for the Aging**, New York, NY
  Participant, Friendly Visitor Program
- **NYC School Volunteer Program**, New York, NY
  Tutor

THE SKILLS-BASED FORMAT

The skills-based format is predicated on a logic which stresses the importance of what you can do rather than where and when you did it. Your qualifications are grouped into skill-based categories such as marketing, counseling, or research that relate directly to the position for which you are applying. The abilities you present on a skills-based resume can be extracted from a wide range of experiences, not just the workplace. For the skills-based resume to be successful, the categories you choose must mirror what the employer is seeking. If the employer is looking for someone with budgeting, negotiation, and public speaking skills, and you stress your management, communication, and planning skills, then it's "bye bye resume." On the other hand, if your categories are on target you have an excellent chance of getting a job interview.

The skills-based format affords tremendous flexibility. It enables you to tailor your qualifications precisely to the needs of the employer. If you know they are looking for someone to write, edit, and conduct research, you simply group your qualifications into those headings (assuming you have those abilities). The skills-based approach is a particularly good choice for those who have limited, irrelevant, or spotty work histories because it glosses over gaps, career shifts, and lack of direct experience. This format also works well for those who have acquired the bulk of their credentials from non-professional experiences such as volunteering, interning, taking classes, and traveling. Finally, it is a good choice for the job seeker who has held several similar positions over the course of a career, and performed the same responsibilities repeatedly. A skills-based approach would enable such a job seeker to avoid the redundancy that would occur in a reverse-chronological format.

Let's consider the case of Evan Rogers, a recent graduate who is not quite sure of the career direction he would like to take. Evan is currently working as a youth counselor, but would prefer to get involved in program development or social science research. His professional experience is fairly limited, and most of his accomplishments have come from a wide range of extracurricular activities. For Evan, a reverse-chronological format would only serve to emphasize the fact that he has limited professional experience and a checkered work history. To avoid giving this impression, Evan thought long and hard about what he would most like to do on his next job, and decided that he would like to use his organizational, leadership, and research skills. He then selected accomplishments pertaining to these areas from his work, school, and extracurricular activities, and sorted them accordingly. He finished the resume with a summary of his work history so the employer could place his experience in a historical context.

The major downside of the skills-based format is that most employers often find it more difficult and time-consuming to read. They also may suspect that if you use this type of resume you are trying to hide some gross deficiency or horrible skeleton in your closet. And let's face it, sometimes you are.

SKILLS-BASED FORMAT CHECKLIST

Consider using this format if:
1. you have limited direct experience in your chosen field
2. your skills have been acquired through study, travel, volunteering, or interning
3. your work history is inconsistent
4. you are changing careers
5. your work experience is repetitive or redundant

SKILLS-BASED FORMAT

Evan Rogers
West Street, Apt. A
Iowa City, IA 30024
(111) 777-7777

EDUCATION   Bachelor of Arts, History, May 1994
University of Iowa, Iowa City, IA
Minor: Mathematics

- Financed approximately 1/3 of college expenses through various part-time and full-time positions including Bartender, Bellhop, and Roofer's Helper.

Activities

- Rugby Club, President
- Iowa Rugby All-Star Team, Member
- Judicial Review Board Committee, Member
- Academic Affairs Search Committee, Member

ORGANIZATIONAL SKILLS

- Procured and managed annual Rugby Club budget of $50,000.
- Coordinated fundraisers, special events, and other activities, including the annual food drive to benefit St. John's/St. Anne's Center, team tours of San Diego and Ireland, and a concert featuring Ukraine's Leontovych String Quartet. Contacted colleges throughout the Northeast to arrange rugby matches.
- Negotiated to bring musical acts Bim Skala Bim and The Mighty Mighty Bosstones to the Spring Weekend '92 Concert.

LEADERSHIP

- Provided general guidance and counseling to educationally and economically disadvantaged 14-17 year-olds.
- Elected Rugby Club President for two consecutive years.
Recruited new members, solidifying the club's position as the largest on campus. Assisted captain with running practices.

RESEARCH SKILLS

- Conducted a comprehensive review of the varying ideologies underlying the state of Iowa's educational policies regarding minorities since 1954. Submitted findings in a 15 page report to the Iowa Education Department's Office of Equity and Access.
- Reviewed and summarized the judicial board policies of other liberal arts colleges for the Dean of Student Affairs.

EMPLOYMENT HISTORY

1993 - Present	Youth Division Aide, Iowa Division for Youth
1993	Intern, Iowa Education Department
1990 - 1992	Various Positions, Mohonk Mountain House

ALTERNATIVE FORMATS

These are basically variations on the reverse-chronological and skills-based themes. They have been created by borrowing elements from one approach and integrating them into the other. If you like taking risks and want to try something a little different, then consider the following formats:

1. The Targeted Reverse-Chronological Format

This format is ideal for the person who has work experience relevant to their career objective, but whose most recent experience is not within their targeted field. By creating targeted experience headings, this approach will enable you to emphasize your most relevant experience and avoid an unfavorable chronology.

Consider the resume of Ray Copper. Ray is in his junior year of college and is interested in obtaining an internship with an accounting firm. His most recent experience with New York University's Office of Career Services is not as relevant to his career objective as some of his prior work experience. To avoid leading off his resume with the NYU position, Ray creates the heading "Business Experience," which enables him to list his most relevant employment first. The less relevant NYU job is then placed in the section "Additional Work Experience" which appears later in the resume. The major drawback of this approach is that the employer has to wait until the latter part of the resume to find out what you're currently doing.

TARGETED REVERSE-CHRONOLOGICAL FORMAT

RAY L. COPPER
25 Union Square
New York, NY 10003
(212) 999-9999

EDUCATION

New York University, Stern School of Business, New York, NY
B.S., Accounting / Actuarial Science, May 1997

Honors: Stern Scholarship for Academic Excellence

Nassau Community College, Garden City, NY
A.A.S., Accounting, December 1993

Overall GPA: 3.88

Honors: Phi Theta Kappa
National Honor Society

BUSINESS EXPERIENCE

1992-1994

H & R Block/VITA, Valley Stream, NY
Tax Preparer

- Prepared individual income tax returns for a highly diverse clientele, including the economically disadvantaged.
- Acquired substantial knowledge of tax laws and IRS procedures.

1989-1991

Custodial Trust Company, Princeton, NJ
Assistant Accountant

- Analyzed financial statements, reconciled bank and general ledger accounts, and investment funds.
- Collaborated on the design of a new billing system.
- Billed clients, and accurately maintained their accounts.
- Computed net equity reports and trading funds.

1989

Whitehorse Savings and Loan, Mercerville, NJ
Bank Teller

- Efficiently and courteously satisfied customers' banking needs in this heavy-volume, high-pressure environment.
- Diplomatically handled account inquiries and expeditiously resolved discrepancies.
- Handled a high volume of requests for cash disbursements, cash receipts, certified checks, opening and closing accounts, and vault and draw audits.

ADDITIONAL WORK EXPERIENCE

1994-Present

New York University Office of Career Services, New York, NY
Administrative Assistant

- Provide administrative support to the Director.
- Maintain and update various databases.
- Oversee alumni billing.

COMPUTER SKILLS

Excel, Lotus 1-2-3, Q & A, Filemaker Pro 2.0, Paradox, DOS, BMDP, Statistix, WordPerfect 5.1, Microsoft Word 5.1

2. The Reverse-Chronological Format with a Skills-Based Twist

This approach is especially effective if you want to stay within the safe confines of the reverse-chronological format, but also want to highlight certain abilities. To do this simply insert skills-based sidebars or subheadings into each job description. This will clue the employer in on what you believe to be your most marketable strengths.

Bruce Rit opted to use this approach because he wanted prospective employers to focus on both his skills and his solid employment history. Bruce was in the process of completing a double Master's degree in the fields of social work and non-profit management. He was seeking a managerial position at a non-profit organization that would enable him to use his strongest abilities: marketing, public relations, fund-raising, program development, and counseling.

Bruce begins his resume with a summary statement to give the reader an overall sense of his background and capabilities. For each of his three most relevant positions, Bruce sorts his accomplishments and responsibilities into the five aforementioned categories. Fortunately, all of this experience fits very neatly into these categories. Otherwise, Bruce would have had two choices: omit the experience, or create a new category.

After thoroughly describing his most relevant experience, Bruce briefly mentions his other work experience to show the reader that he's not a one-dimensional candidate. Lastly, Bruce prioritizes the subheadings within each job according to their degree of marketability. Naturally, the order could be easily changed if he were to apply for positions with different requirements.

Reverse-Chronological Format with a Skills-Based Twist

Bruce Rit
Maple Street • Burlington, VT 00011 • (666) 666-6666

SUMMARY

Extensive experience in a variety of non-profit organizations with proven ability in fund-raising, marketing, public relations, program development, and counseling.

EDUCATION

University of Vermont, Burlington, VT
Masters of Social Work and Masters of Science in Non-Profit Management, May 1996

University of Maryland, College Park, MD
Bachelor of Science, Business and Marketing, Cum Laude, December 1986

NON-PROFIT EXPERIENCE

FOUNDER, B.A.G.A.L., Brattleboro, VT   1992-1993
Marketing/Fund-raising
Initiated and implemented various development activities including special events, direct mail, advertising sales, and community solicitation. Increased membership by 200 %.

Public Relations
Established, developed, and maintained positive working relationships with various community organizations resulting in increased public awareness of and support for the organization. Designed promotional materials. Published a statewide newsletter.

CONSULTANT, Brattleboro AIDS Project, Brattleboro, VT   1991-1992
Public Relations/Fund-raising
Enhanced public relations through expanded community outreach, increased media contact, and the redesign of promotional materials. Planned special events; helped write grants; raised funds through community solicitation and the initiation of fee-based services.

Program Development
Gathered and analyzed data on trends regarding the transmission of HIV/AIDS. Developed and implemented community AIDS educational campaigns.

CASEWORKER, The Brattleboro Retreat, Brattleboro, VT   1990-1991
Counseling
Developed and coordinated treatment plans as part of a multi-disciplinary team. Direct clinical experience with a diverse case load of patients in recovery from substance abuse.

Program Development
Designed and implemented Stress Reduction and Journal Writing programs for patients.

ADDITIONAL EXPERIENCE

MARKETING ASSISTANT, Patriot Bank   1988-1990

ASSISTANT MANAGER, Appalachian Mountain Club   1987-1988

SKILLS

Conversant in Spanish, WordPerfect 5.1

3. Skills-Based Format with Employer Headings

A third alternative resume format option is to use the skills-based approach, but to indicate the name of the employer next to each accomplishment. This technique should make life a bit easier for the reader since they will no longer have to guess about what happened where. However, by adding employer headings you will be left with less space on the page, and thus may be forced to do some creative editing.

The resume of Clancy Ruiz points out the advantages and disadvantages of this approach. Clancy's goal is to use his writing/editing and administrative skills within a community-based organization. The skills-based format was appropriate for Clancy since his skills are rather impressive, whereas a historical review of his work experience would probably leave the employer dazed and confused. Adding the employer headings to each accomplishment helps to contextualize Clancy's experience for the reader. All the added information also has the negative side effect of cluttering the resume, forcing Clancy to use small print and a layout that maximizes the use of space.

Skills-Based Format with Employer Headings

CLANCY RUIZ

8th Street • San Diego, CA 11111 • (888) 888-8888

EDUCATION

University of California at San Diego (UCSD), *B.A., English*, May 1995, Overall GPA: 3.3
 • Financed college education through full-time employment while attending classes

WRITING / EDITING EXPERIENCE

Clearwater Revival
 Write artist bios for annual environmental festival; interview sloop club directors.

Women's Action Coalition
 Assisted with writing a press release concerning the definition of women in the '90s.

Ultracomputer Research Laboratory
 Assist Director with editing academic papers prior to journal submission; edit papers of graduate students for clarity and style.

COMMUNITY SERVICE

Grace Opportunity Project
 Tutor fourth grade Latino students in reading, math, and writing.

UCSD AHANA Mentor
 Mentored incoming NYU minority underclassmen to help ease their transition to college.

UCSD Higher Education Opportunities Program
 Inform educators in alternative high schools of higher education opportunities for their students.

ADMINISTRATION

Ultracomputer Research Laboratory
 Maintain and format on-line resource library on Unix system. Manage office operations.

Department of Human Services and Education/Resource Access Project
 Played major role in assembling 600+ person conferences; attended conferences and ensured that they operated smoothly; trained users on various software applications.

Computerland
 Assisted director of finance in all phases of transition to an on-line in-house payroll system.

PROFESSIONAL EXPERIENCE

 • Ultracomputer Research Laboratory, 1991-Present
 • Department of Human Services and Education, Resource Access Project, 1989-1991
 • Computerland, 1988

SKILLS

 • **IBM**: DBase IV, Lotus 1-2-3, Wordperfect, LAN • **Macintosh**: Microsoft Word • **UNIX**: troff, vi, tbl,eqn
 • Fluent in written and conversational Spanish. Working knowledge of French.

CHAPTER 4

RESUME LANGUAGE

KEEP IT SIMPLE

Remember English Composition? How you slaved over every assignment to write the prose of your life? As you sit down to write your resume, you can forget most of what you learned. The best resumes violate practically all the rules your professors struggled so hard to teach.

Your goal in writing a resume is to make the reader's job as easy as possible. Write in the active voice in a straightforward, economical style. Keep your sentences relatively short and to the point. Personal pronouns are unnecessary, because they are implied. Helping and being verbs are too passive—you can eliminate them as well. If you're running out of space on the page, you can also get rid of most articles. Finally, avoid cryptic abbreviations and obscure acronyms. Spell out everything so the employer knows what you're talking about.

Eliminate Personal Pronouns

Supervised 12 peer counselors.

instead of

I supervised 12 peer counselors.

Eliminate Helping/Being Verbs

Produced a benefit concert for victims of Hurricane Bill.

instead of

Was responsible for producing a benefit concert for victims of Hurricane Bill.

Use language that is readily comprehensible to the layperson, but demonstrates your familiarity with the buzzwords and terms commonly used in your prospective field. For example, if you're a lawyer you meet with "clients." If you're a sales representative you handle "accounts." If you're a programmer you deal with "end users." The idea is to employ language that proves to industry insiders that you know your stuff. On the other hand, don't let your resume become so jargon-laden that it can only be understood by a specialist.

Results Rule

The most difficult part of resume writing is describing your experiences. The most effective approach is to begin each job description with a power verb. *Improved*, *increased*, and *attained* are all examples of power verbs. They stress results, which are, after all, what employers care about most. Leading off with a power verb will catch the reader's attention and draw them into your description. Depending on the accomplishment you're trying to describe, you can string together two or more power verbs to add some extra punch to your description. Two of our favorite power strings are, *designed*, *developed*, and *implemented*, and *established*, *cultivated*, and *maintained*.

You can make your description come alive by quantifying or qualifying the object of your action. Employers aren't just interested in what you did . . . they also want to know how well and how much. In some instances it is difficult, if not impossible, to describe your work in qualitative or quantitative terms. In this case, simply state what you did and leave it at that. Refrain from adding fluff or embellishment. Nothing will turn off an employer faster.

Quantification

Provided customer service to over 200,000 callers annually.

instead of

Provided customer service to callers.

Qualification

Resolved staff-management conflicts in a diplomatic and sensitive manner.

instead of

Resolved staff-management conflicts.

The tricky part is finding just the right words to communicate your abilities and accomplishments. Try varying your language as much as possible. Too much repetition will lull your reader to sleep. Keep a thesaurus by your side as you write, along with this handy list of power verbs.

Power Verbs That Demonstrate Leadership, Decision Making, or Management Skills

Allocated funds for various Karate Club projects.

Determined club policy regarding the admission of new members.

Directed a team of five oceanographers seeking the lost city of Atlantis.

Elected President of Psychic Club for three consecutive years.

Enlisted the support of 20 volunteers to restore a community garden.

Formed a student committee to investigate the abuse of alcohol on campus.

Founded a volunteer organization dedicated to serving the needs of the homeless.

Governed the University Senate, adhering to the highest standards of honesty and integrity.

Hired a staff of 15 phone interviewers for the alumni telethon.

Initiated the unionization of domestic workers, including housewives.

Inspired obese individuals to adopt a low-fat vegetarian diet.

Instituted a more relaxed dress code to boost staff morale.

Led foreign visitors on a walking tour of lower Manhattan.

Managed an exclusive hair salon catering to entertainment personalities.

Moderated a panel discussion on the impact of nuclear proliferation.

Motivated volunteers to work extra shifts prior to the mayoral election.

Operated a successful computer graphics consulting firm for three years.

Oversaw the distribution of refreshments to more than 5,000 marathoners.

Pioneered the national anti-fraternity movement.

Presided over monthly student council meetings.

Produced an orientation video for New York University Office of Career Services.

Recruited, hired, and trained ten new staff members.

Represented the student body on the Faculty Recruitment Coordinating Committee.

Selected bands for the Senior Week Celebration.

Spearheaded efforts to ban the use of animals in laboratory experiments.

Sponsored a bill to make all tuition benefits tax-exempt.

Staged a benefit concert for victims of Hurricane Bill.

Started a campus-based travel agency designed to serve the university community.

Supervised 12 peer counselors.

Power Verbs That Demonstrate Administrative, Organizational, and Follow-Through Skills

Arranged transportation to and from conference site for over 100 visiting scholars.

Assembled press kits and promotional packages for national rock and roll music tours.

Collected delinquent payments from patients.

Centralized alumni credential files resulting in more efficient file maintenance.

Coordinated seating arrangements at fashion shows for media and retailers.

Catalogued the private art collection of David Byrne.

Distributed a weekly newsletter to 4,000 subscribers.

Disseminated pamphlets on HIV to Residence Life staff members.

Enforced the laws of New York State in the most equitable manner possible.

Executed stock and option orders issued by retail brokers.

Formalized application procedures for the Alumni Mentor Program.

Implemented a computerized registration system.

Installed system software on over 250 computer stations.

Maintained a comprehensive log of acceptable sound takes.

Organized a ski trip to Utah during winter break.

Planned a twelve-part lecture series concerning international politics.

Prepared a list of low cost treatment centers throughout the city.

Processed over 100 financial aid applications daily.

Routed over 500 calls daily to a staff of twenty-five.

Recorded minutes at weekly staff meetings.

Reorganized the Career Resource Center collection based on the Holland codes.

Scheduled weekly social outings for dormitory residents.

Updated alumni mailing list for annual fundraising drive.

Power Verbs That Demonstrate Communication Skills

Acquainted Swiss diplomats with the cultural attractions of New York City.

Apprised management of shifts in consumer buying patterns.

Answered callers' questions during an alternative music radio talk show.

Briefed reporters on recent developments in United States foreign policy.

Conducted campus tours for prospective students and their parents.

Contacted subscribers by phone to offer a special renewal rate.

Demonstrated how to use Word 5.1 to create an in-house newsletter.

Drafted correspondence for senior management.

Educated parents of the physically challenged about the *Americans with Disabilities Act.*

Explained academic requirements to incoming freshmen at the College of Arts and Science.

Familiarized Rwandan refugees with American customs and practices.

Handled phone requests for tickets to events at Foxboro Stadium.

Informed committee members of the various factors affecting student retention.

Instructed a group of inner-city junior high school students in the basics of photography.

Introduced guest speakers during Career Week panel discussions.

Lectured American physicians about the benefits of Eastern healing practices.

Listened to employee grievances.

Presented major selling points of the new swimwear collection to sales force.

Reported findings about campus safety to the Executive Committee.

Responded to phone inquiries regarding the admissions process.

Spoke about the relationship between diet and overall health at the AMA conference.

Summarized the judicial board policies of fifteen liberal arts colleges.

Taught basic English to children of Mexican migrant workers.

Trained bartenders on how to properly mix "Sex on the Beach."

Translated romance novels from English to Spanish.

Wrote a daily summary of the New York Stock Exchange activity.

Power Verbs That Demonstrate Analytical or Research Skills

Analyzed blood samples to determine cholesterol levels.

Assessed clients' readiness to return to the workplace.

Audited financial records of the Board of Education.

Compiled a critical bibliography of contemporary Brazilian music.

Consulted on the design of a virtual reality installation.

Detected signs of intelligent life beyond the universe.

Discovered a new species of reptile in the Amazon.

Documented the history of soccer in Eastern Europe.

Edited manuscripts for content and style.

Evaluated job readiness of newly arrived immigrants.

Examined supermarket poultry to determine salmonella bacteria levels.

Gathered data on violent crime trends in the United States.

Identified students in need of remedial help.

Interpreted entertainment contracts and prepared contract amendments.

Interviewed varsity basketball players for a feature article in *The Targum*.

Researched the relationship between income level and political affiliation.

Searched NHL archives for information on hockey in the United States before 1920.

Surveyed over 2,000 Alabama residents to determine their opinions on television violence.

Tested the effects of marijuana on short-term memory.

Power Verbs that Demonstrate the Ability to Create or Innovate

Authored two articles about psychic phenomena.

Conceived of the international blockbuster film, *Transvestites in Turkey*.

Conceptualized a twelve-step program for chocolate addicts.

Created in-store displays utilizing glow-in-the-dark mannequins.

Composed a film score for a documentary on the Russian Revolution.

Designed a five week intensive Spanish conversation course for hospital personnel.

Devised a direct marketing campaign for a non-dairy frozen dessert.

Established long-term objectives for a national community service initiative.

Invented a solar powered light bulb capable of illuminating a 300-square foot room.

Originated the "Fashion Compassion Ball," an annual fundraiser for battered women.

Revolutionized the use of Styrofoam models in print advertising.

Power Verbs That Demonstrate Counseling, Helping, or Mediating Skills

Aided the homeless with all aspects of their job search.

Attended to the daily needs of nursing home residents.

Assisted students with the career decision-making process.

Collaborated on the design of a new billing system.

Contributed to the development of the restaurant's new outdoor seating area.

Counseled college seniors on the transition from school to work.

Comforted children suffering from various serious illnesses.

Facilitated the installation of a multimedia exhibit honoring female athletes.

Fostered the reconciliation between African-American and Jewish residents in Crown Heights.

Guided high school students through the college application process.

Helped victims of child abuse regain their self-esteem.

Instilled confidence in individuals trying to overcome their fear of flying.

Mentored high school students considering careers in physical therapy.

Provided warmth and companionship to children suffering from leukemia.

Settled disagreements between landlords and tenants.

Supported sales efforts of brokers by maintaining up-to-date client records.

Tutored elementary school students in basic math.

Treated patients with multiple psychological disorders.

Power Verbs That Demonstrate the Ability to Convince or Sell

Arbitrated a settlement between team owners and players.

Convinced owner to introduce daily drink specials resulting in a twenty percent increase in profits.

Dissuaded union members from voting in favor of a walkout.

Encouraged dormitory residents to participate in weekly "town hall" meetings.

Marketed carpentry services via phone and direct mail.

Mediated conflicts between quarreling roommates.

Negotiated contracts on behalf of 1,200 union members.

Persuaded shoppers to sample perfumes and cologne.

Promoted long distance telephone services to businesses in the New York metropolitan area.

Publicized film screenings via flyers, posters, and ads in the local paper.

Resolved disputes between management and staff concerning salary increases.

Sold advertising space to clothing retailers throughout California.

Secured new accounts by making in-person sales presentations.

Solicited alumni for contributions to restore the damaged cathedral.

Some More Useful Power Verbs

Adapted teaching style to meet the needs of inner-city youth.

Attained the level of black belt after three months of intensive karate lessons.

Augmented sales by 25% through extensive phone follow-up.

Awarded the Anderson Medal for superior sportsmanship.

Boosted net retail sales by 50% over the last quarter.

Broadened awareness of Middle Eastern politics through extensive travel.

Built temporary housing for the homeless.

Calculated daily shifts in foreign exchange rates.

Catered awards ceremonies for up to 3,000 attendees.

Decreased the average wait for registration by 25%.

Developed expertise on the subject of vintage French wines.

Ensured customer accounts complied with Federal Reserve regulations.

Eliminated dangerous admission rites for newly accepted fraternity brothers.

Exceeded monthly sales quotas a record 15 consecutive times.

Excelled at providing professional, courteous, and efficient service.

Expanded retail operations to 50 sites nationwide.

Expedited the processing of transcript requests.

Fabricated all molds and tools by hand.

Financed 75% of college education through full-time work.

Gained experience with a variety of desktop publishing programs.

Generated significant student interest in CIEE's work abroad programs.

Improved relations between staff and management through monthly gripe sessions.

Increased paid membership by 200% within two years.

Launched a campus-wide public relations campaign for the Schick Tracer.

Mastered spoken Greek while traveling throughout Crete.

Modernized the recreation center by introducing the latest line of Nautilus machines.

Published a monthly newsletter listing internship opportunities nationwide.

Raised the ability and confidence level of beginning racquetball players.

Reconciled out-of-balance expense accounts.

Reduced campus waste by introducing a dorm-based recycling plan.

Revamped the school library, making it accessible to those with impaired mobility.

Revitalized cheerleading squad through modernized costumes and dance routines.

Saved employer $20,000 by revamping vendor system.

Shopped retail establishments to determine current fashion trends.

Strengthened business relationships by providing superior customer service.

Supplemented lectures with role plays and interactive group exercises.

Tended bar at an exclusive Soho drinking establishment.

Utilized spreadsheet software to aid with line planning.

CHAPTER 5

THE GREAT RESUME DEBATE

WHO DO YOU TRUST?

Over the years we've encountered career counselors, writers, former human resource professionals, and outplacement executives who claim to have the last word on resumes. We have read many of their books and have been impressed with what they had to say. These self-proclaimed gurus promise that if you follow their advice, you'll end up with a winning resume. In the back of our minds we've always wondered if the people who have the last word on resumes—the employers—agree with their advice.

To answer this question, we administered a questionnaire to over a hundred recruiters at some of the nation's top corporations spanning the fields of accounting, banking, computer science, consulting, consumer products, education, health care, hospitality, insurance, manufacturing, marketing, publishing, and retail. Simultaneously, we administered the same questionnaire to over a hundred career development professionals working in settings such as colleges, outplacement firms, non-profit organizations, and private practice. The questionnare included a broad range of resume-related issues.

The polls have closed and the results are in. Forty-five corporate recruiters and sixty-four career development professionals completed the survey for a response rate of nearly fifty percent. Let's see what they had to say.

Question #1: What Are Three Key Ingredients of a Successful Resume?

The career development folks and the recruiters all agreed on this one. Recruiters cited readability, overall presentation, and conciseness as the three keys to a successful resume. Incidentally, all three of these qualities make the recruiter's job easier. Makes sense when you consider the thousands of resumes they have to sift through.

Career counselors also cited readability, presentation, and conciseness as the three main keys to a good resume. In addition, they emphasized that the resume should be tailored to fit the requirements of the job and that it should stress notable accomplishments and results in your former jobs, not just job descriptions. Recruiters generally agreed with this advice.

Resume Keys	Recruiters	Counselors
Readability	38%	56%
Presentation	27%	41%
Conciseness	24%	30%
Results	18%	28%
Tailored to Opening	13%	28%

Question #2: What Are the Three Most Common Resume Mistakes Made by College Students?

Again, our two groups of respondents were basically in agreement. Employers cited sloppiness, wordiness, and omitting grade point average as the three top resume killers. They found typos, misspellings, and grammatical mistakes to be especially irksome. In their eyes, a resume with these careless errors is simply unprofessional. Employers assume that if you make thoughtless blunders on your own resume, you may be equally sloppy on the job.

Fortunately, typos, misspellings, and poor grammar are avoidable mistakes. To ensure that you don't commit these careless errors, always take the following precautions: 1) Keep a dictionary and grammar guide (such as The Princeton Review's *Grammar Smart*) by your side whenever writing a resume; 2) If you have any doubts about how to spell a word, or which preposition to use, consult your handy reference sources; 3) Spell check the entire document on your word processor; 4) Ask two trusted friends who have a good command of the English language to proofread your resume. Proofing it yourself is okay for starters, but an objective third party should always read your final draft.

In our questionnaire, nearly a third of the employers cited wordiness as one of the most common resume mistakes. Just because a sentence is long doesn't mean it's good. In fact, on your resume the more long-winded you are, the less likely you are to hold your audience's attention. The idea is to get to the point. Remember, your resume is just a summary of your experience—you can supply the gory details during the interview. Also keep in mind that you can only squeeze around 250 words onto a standard one-page resume. Therefore, every word should be chosen with great care and consideration, and for a specific purpose. If a word doesn't enhance the way you look on paper, don't use it. Consider the following example:

Original Version

I compiled information and wrote the first draft for a launch book introducing the first sinus-relief product with daytime and nightime formulations in a single package.

Revised Version

Completed draft of launch book introducing a unique sinus relief product.

Note that the personal pronoun "I" and several articles ("the," "a,") have been omitted to unclutter the statement. Editing has reduced the new version to from two lines of text to one—quite significant in a one-page resume of thirty-three lines. Just think: each line you waste with wordiness is equivalent to approximately three percent of your life. Waste three lines and you've just flushed nearly ten percent of your life down the drain.

The third most common resume mistake according to employers—omitting GPA—was somewhat unexpected. While recruiters in many fields use grade point average as an initial criterion for job qualification, in certain fields, GPA is a lesser or irrelevant factor. (More about this later.)

Unlike recruiters, career counselors were not dismayed by the omission of GPA. In fact, many counselors actually encourage students to omit GPA, particularly when it is below a 3.0.

A fourth common resume mistake that really bothered the counselors was lack of career focus. Interestingly, this did not seem to be an area of concern for the recruiters. Perhaps they take it for granted that many students have little idea what they want to do with their lives.

Common Mistakes	Recruiters	Counselors
Sloppiness	56%	39%
Wordiness	29%	22%
Omitting GPA	20%	0%
Unfocused	0%	25%

Question #3: Which Resume Format Do You Prefer?

Among the recruiters, more than three quarters preferred the reverse-chronological format. It is the easiest format to read. A few recruiters favored the functional approach, and a few didn't really care as long as the candidate communicates her qualifications clearly.

The career counselors were not quite as uniform in their opinion, although more than half preferred the reverse-chronological style. Those who preferred the functional format said it was particularly effective for students with little or no work experience, older students with varied backgrounds, career changers, and job hunters with erratic work histories. Counselors also pointed out that writing a functional resume is an excellent exercise in skills assessment that requires the writer articulate what he does best.

Nearly a quarter of the counselors stated that the choice of format depended on the client's individual circumstances. About one in ten counselors favored alternative approaches, including the combination format and the targeted format. The combination format integrates elements of the reverse-chronological and functional styles, while the targeted format highlights accomplishments and skills that are particularly relevant to the job sought.

Preferred Resume Format	Recruiters	Counselors
Reverse-Chronological	78%	56%
Functional	10%	8%
No Preference	7%	2%
Depends	2.5%	23%
Other	2.5%	11%

Question #4: Should an Applicant List GPA

Three quarters of the corporate recruiters answered a resounding, "Yes!" Grade point average is used by employers in many industries as a job-screening mechanism: if you're above the GPA cutoff, you're still in the running . . . if you're below it, you're out. Those who advocated listing GPA pointed out that when GPA is omitted, the recruiter may assume that the applicant's grades are lower than they really are. Recruiters also recommended that students should indicate the scale being used when listing GPA (e.g., 3.5/4.0).

Resume Bloopers

SPECIAL AREAS OF INTEREST: Drug law reform

Sixteen percent of the recruiters said that the decision to list your GPA should be contingent on how high it is. Suggested cutoffs varied from 2.7 to 3.5, with most of the responses hovering around 3.0. The rest of the corporate recruiters advised against listing GPA. Some supported their view by claiming that GPA is not a valid predictor of future job perfomance.

Among the career counselors comments varied considerably. Nearly all of the counselors said that the decision to list GPA should be based on the strength of the applicant's grades. Suggested cutoffs ranged from a low of 2.5 to a high of 3.75, with most counselors citing the magic 3.0 as the minimum acceptable grade for listing on a resume. Some individuals advised that GPA should be listed only for certain industries, such as accounting, consulting, information systems, investment banking, law, and medicine. Others claimed that GPA should only be listed if it is relevant to the position for which a student is applying, or if the applicant has a weak employment history. Counselors opposed to listing GPA stated that academic success can be more effectively conveyed by listing honors such as Phi Beta Kappa, and that GPAs aren't taken seriously because they can be so easily manipulated.

Should GPA Be Listed?	Recruiters	Counselors
Yes	73%	5%
No	11%	11%
Depends	16%	84%

Question #5: Do You Prefer the Use of Bulleted Statements or Paragraphs to Distinguish Job Descriptions?

Three out of four employee recruiters surveyed say, "We prefer bullets." The pro-bulleters argued that bulleted statements are easier to read than paragraphs. The remainder of the recruiters were split between having no preference (fourteen percent) and preferring paragraphs (thirteen percent).

Counselors also showed a strong preference for bullets. Many pointed out, though, that because bulleted statements take up more space on a page than paragraphs, the decision is often dictated by design considerations. Those in favor of bullets maintained that paragraphs often get too wordy. A few counselors said they preferred bullets for describing notable accomplishments, and paragraphs for summarizing job responsiblities. Those counselors who preferred paragraphs claimed that they convey more information than bulleted statements.

Bullets vs. Paragraphs	Recruiters	Counselors
Bullets	73%	64%
Paragraphs	13%	5%
No preference	14%	3%
Depends	0%	23%
Combination approach	0%	5%

Question #6: Should An Applicant Include Interests On His Resume?

Unexpectedly, over seventy percent of the recruiters said, 'Yes!" and most frequently offered two reasons to support their opinion. First, recruiters said they like to ease into interviews by asking applicants about their interests. This tactic serves as an icebreaker and tends to relax both interviewer and interviewee. Second, interests can reveal a lot about an individual—whether he is well-rounded, for example. Some employers cautioned, however, that if you do choose to list interests, make the list short and the interests unique or relevant to the job.

In support of listing interests on a resume, one counselor observed that most students are questioned about their interests on an interview. Another counselor pointed out that listing interests is a way to indicate that you are a healthy, well-balanced, multi-faceted individual. The counselors opposed to listing interests claimed that interests are often irrelevant or boring.

List Interests	Recruiters	Counselors
Yes	38%	56%
No	27%	41%
If relevant/unique	24%	30%
No preference	18%	28%

Question #7: Should an Applicant State Her Job Objective?

Over sixty percent of the recruiters said, "Yes," while a little less than a quarter said, "No." Others said don't bother listing an objective unless it's focused. Recruiters in favor commented that by defining an objective, a student sends the message that he is goal-oriented. Those opposed pointed out that the objective can be more appropriately defined in the cover letter or discussed during the interview. One recruiter said that it doesn't really matter whether or not an objective is on the resume—he never reads the objective statement anyway.

Forty percent of the career counselors felt the decision to list an objective should be based on how focused it is and how much space is available on the resume. Nearly the same percentage advocated an objective statement without qualifying in which cases this would be appropriate. Those opposed to objective statements on a resume suggested placement in the cover letter. One counselor commented that most objectives tend to sound like "tepid dish water," and therefore aren't worth including. Another recommended preparing two resumes, one with an objective and one without. Others advocated the use of a summary statement or profile in place of an objective.

State Objective	Recruiters	Counselors
Yes	62%	38%
No	22%	22%
Depends	16%	40%

Question #8: Should an Applicant Indicate That References Are Available on Request?

Three quarters of the recruiters and counselors agreed that this is not necessary, but that the job hunter should always bring a list of references to the interview. Several respondents said they assume that references are available whether or not they are mentioned on the resume. They suggested using the line for something more important.

A lesser but significant number of respondents indicated that job applicants gain credibility by indicating that they have references. Others said that "References available on request" signals the end of the resume and serves to visually balance the page.

Mention References	Recruiters	Counselors
Yes	14%	22%
No	86%	72%
Depends	0%	6%

CHAPTER 6

THE COMPLETE RESUME

You are about to embark on a guided tour of Resumania—a planet where many have boldly gone before, only to be lost forever in time and space . . . a planet with a land mass of 93.5 square inches whose inhabitants can only survive in two dimensions . . . a destination somewhere between reality and fantasy where the lines between past, present, and future often fade into nothingness.

BEFORE THE TOUR BEGINS

Resumania can be a dangerous place, especially after 2 A.M., but if you promise to do the following we assure you no harm will come.

1. Stay close to your escort throughout the tour and heed his instructions in case of emergency.
2. Grab a pencil and some paper.
3. Review your personal history inventory and keep it handy.
4. Reacquaint yourself with the various resume format options presented in chapter 3 and decide which one is best for you.
5. Buckle up your seatbelt and get ready for the adventure of a lifetime. You're about to start writing your resume.

WHAT'S IN A NAME?

Your name is the very first thing an employer should see on your resume. Do not place the word "resume" at the top of your resume or any other inane introduction like "Qualifications of Mortimer Jones." If the employer can't tell it's a resume from looking at it, then you need to go back to the drawing board.

If presented properly, your name should make a positive and lasting impression. The way your name appears on the page says a great deal about your self-image, and employers can often pick up on this vibe. Is your name printed in microscopic letters, or is it three inches tall? Is it in a classic or flashy typeface? Is it in all caps, title case, toggle case, or lowercase? Consider the following inappropriate examples:

Your name generally looks best when it is either centered or pulled out to the left hand margin. Make it slightly larger than anything else on your resume. If you're using 12 point type, then see how your name looks at 14 points. You might even want to go a bit larger depending on the typeface you've selected, but usually 18 points is the limit. Larger than that and your name is no longer big, it's obnoxious. Using bold print and all caps can help make your name stand out even more, but this is optional.

Should you list your full name or a shortened version? Base your decision on the image you want to project. Do you want to come across as extremely formal or kind of casual? Your strategy may vary according to the audience being targeted. What is your gut reaction to the three following approaches? Go with what feels right.

Most formal	**TIMOTHY DLYN HAFT**
Less formal	**TIMOTHY D. HAFT**
Casual	**TIM HAFT**

Sounds Like . . .

If you have a non-English first name that's difficult to pronounce, you may want to add an English equivalent in parentheses so the interviewer will be able to address you without embarrassment. Or, if you want to avoid generating suspicion that you might be an international (non-citizen) student, you could use only your English name. For example:

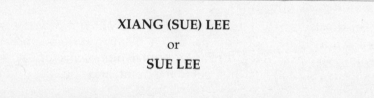

XIANG (SUE) LEE
or
SUE LEE

Mr. or Ms.?

Gender-neutral names present similar difficulties for employers, particularly in making phone calls to the applicant or in properly addressing correspondence. If using your full middle name or slightly modifying your first name will clarify the situation, it may be worth doing. Of course, once the interviewer meets you she'll know your gender, so don't sweat it.

Address and Phone Number

You should list your complete address and phone number (except actors applying for performance jobs, who can get away with just a phone number) as well as your fax number, if you have one. Keep in mind, however, that good news usually comes by phone and bad news by mail.

If the mail sent to your dormitory is circulated to everyone else before it gets to you, then think about listing the address of a trusted family member or friend. Getting a P.O. box is also an option, but a post office address may imply transience. If you're living at a temporary address, it's a good idea to indicate on the resume how long the address will be valid. And don't forget to list a second address where you can receive mail after you've moved.

You can list either your home phone number, your office number, or both. Obviously, you should only list your office number if the boss knows that you're looking for a job and you've been given the green light to receive calls at work. Otherwise you may find yourself being scolded or getting the boot.

GET THE MESSAGE?

Make sure a reliable person or machine will take messages for you if you're not available. Purchasing an answering machine or signing up for a voice mail or answering service is practically essential for today's job hunter. Speed is of the essence—employers want everything done yesterday. Miss a call and it could cost you a job.

If you do use an answering machine, keep in mind that employers will be forming an opinion of you based on the way you sound and the type of message you leave. Keep it professional. No hardcore music, sound effects, vulgar jokes, or soliloquies. Just get to the point, and speak confidently, slowly, and clearly.

ADDRESS PLACEMENT

On your resume, your address and phone number generally look best centered below your name, with a little space between the two (about four points). This will help make your name stand out. Another option is to center your name, and split your address wide left, and your phone numbers wide right. It's not advisable to use bold print or capital letters for your address and phone number, as you don't want this information to steal the spotlight from your name. Feel free to abbreviate certain words such as street, apartment, or avenue.

1

SUE LEE

666 Nirvana Avenue, Apt. X
Black Hills, SD 11001
Home: 303-444-5555
Office: 303-224-3333

2

SUE LEE

666 Nirvana Avenue, Apt. X
Black Hills, SD 11001

Home: 303-444-5555
Office: 303-224-3333

3

SUE LEE   666 Nirvana Avenue, Apt. X   •   Black Hills, SD 11001   •   Phone/Fax: 303-444- 5555

4

SUE LEE

666 Nirvana Avenue, Apt. X   •   Black Hills, SD 11001   •   303-444-5555

5

SUE LEE

Until May 15, 1995
666 Nirvana Avenue, Apt. X
Black Hills, SD 110011
(303) 444-5555

After May 15, 1995
Rocky Road, #6
Boise, ID 12345
(404) 222-1111

THE PROFILE—YOUR OPENING STATEMENT

Just as the first thirty seconds of an interview set the tone for the remainder of the interview, the first few inches of your resume will often determine whether the rest of it even gets read. You need to make a strong positive impression from the start. One technique that has become increasingly popular is to start the resume with a summary or profile section. This section takes the place of a stated career objective. A profile section is particularly useful for experienced job hunters, and those who need a coherent opening statement to tie together diverse work experiences.

The summary or profile is actually a summary of a summary. It serves as a teaser to whet the appetite of the reader and hopefully intrigue him to read on. It is a sound byte that, in a few carefully composed lines, shows the employer that you understand his needs, and have the goods he is looking for. A profile is probably not necessary if you are an undergraduate, but it can be a powerful tool for grad students and alumni with a few years of experience.

To create your summary you must know what the prospective employer is really looking for in a candidate. More importantly, you must have the qualifications they are seeking. The rest is easy. Try to come up with two to four sentences or bulleted statements that communicate your most relevant credentials. Keep in mind, however, that you will need to modify your summary depending on the requirements of each position for which you are applying. The following examples should help get you started.

Sample Profiles/Summaries

Joan is seeking a position at an advertising agency as an account executive.

SUMMARY	Five years of experience in advertising and related fields, with a strong track record in account management, direct mail, print production, and traffic. Strong communicator with excellent organizational skills. Perform best under deadline pressure.

Marla is hoping to become a craps dealer at a Las Vegas casino.

> **PROFILE**
>
> • Over four years of casino experience in Atlantic City as a floorperson, boxman, and dealer.
>
> • Uphold and maintain the highest standards of ethics and integrity in all business and personal dealings.

Lina is applying for jobs in public relations for the fashion industry.

> **SUMMARY**
>
> Five years of experience in the fashion industry with significant exposure to both wholesale and retail. Expertise in public relations, special events, marketing, and product development. Keen awareness of new trends and styles. Highly organized with a proven ability to meet deadlines.

John is looking into positions in restaurant management.

> **PROFILE**
>
> • Over four years of experience in the food and beverage industry.
>
> • Excel at providing professional, courteous, and efficient service.
>
> • Substantial knowledge of haute cuisine and fine wines.

THE OBJECTIVE

As we learned in chapter 5, over sixty percent of the recruiters surveyed favor the inclusion of an objective. If you choose to list an objective, it should be focused and concise. This is an opportunity to demonstrate to your prospective employer that you really know what you want in a job. Your objective should also be employer-oriented. Don't emphasize what you want to get out of the job, but rather what you can offer the employer.

Although your objective should be focused, if you make it too specific you run the risk of limiting your range of employment options. Occasionally your resume may end up in the hands of an employer who doesn't have a suitable opening but knows a colleague who does. If the objective on your resume isn't too constraining, the employer may pass your resume to a colleague for consideration. On the other hand, if your objective is so broad that it's not saying much of anything, it's better to omit it.

A General Objective

OBJECTIVE	Summer internship in the field of accounting.

A Precise Objective

Objective	Position as a systems analyst in a UNIX environment.

A Targeted Objective Which Demonstrates One's Knowledge and Skills

OBJECTIVE	Paralegal position which requires expertise in legal research, trusts and estates, and patent law, as well as knowledge of Lexis and Westlaw.

A Badly-Phrased Objective

OBJECTIVE	A managerial position affording growth, challenge and opportunity, while enabling me to utilize my interpersonal and communication skills.

EDUCATION

For most of you, this section is a major selling point. It should be placed at the top of your resume, just below your objective or summary statement, if you have one. The exception is if you have a great deal of experience in your field, as with "returning students" or recent alumni who have already made their professional debut. In this case, your experience section should come first. You might also want to deemphasize education if it is irrelevant to the field you are entering, or could in some way be considered a liability. For example, if you are seeking a position in restaurant management, it is likely that employers in this field will be more interested in your hands-on restaurant experience than the fact that you have an M.A. in philosophy.

The education section consists of the following: the institution you attended; the city and state in which it's located (you don't have to list this if it's obvious); the name of the degree, diploma, or certificate you received; your field of study; and the month and year of graduation. If you've been out of school awhile, listing the year of graduation without the month is fine. If you are still in school, don't feel compelled to say "anticipated" or "expected" before you list your degree date. The fact that the date is in the future makes it obvious that the degree is expected.

Basic Education Layout

EDUCATION	**Northwestern University**, Evanston, IL B.A., *English*, May 1995

Double Major Layout

Education

NEW YORK UNIVERSITY, New York, NY
Bachelor of Science, **Finance and Accounting**, December 1995

Space-saving Layout

EDUCATION	**School of Visual Arts** • *B.F.A.*, *Photography*, May 1995

Minor Consequences

You can also list your minor, as well as any other additional concentration of course work that you think would interest an employer. And for those of you who financed all or part of your education, you can add a line to convey this fact, such as "financed 75% of college expenses through part-time work as a waiter, bartender, and messenger." This demonstrates to employers that you are multi-dimensional and have a strong work ethic.

Education

1

NEW YORK UNIVERSITY, New York, NY
Bachelor of Arts, *Anthropology*, December 1995
Minor: *Sociology*
Additional concentration in *European History* and *20th Century Philosophy*

---

2 EDUCATION **Northwestern University**, Evanston, IL
B.A., *English*, May 1995

• Financed 75% of college costs through part-time work.

You Went to Whatchamacallit State?

The order in which you list your school and degree depends on what you feel makes you most marketable. If you went to a big name school that you think might open some doors, then list the name of the institution first. On the other hand, if you went to an obscure school where you received a highly marketable degree, then list your degree first. If you went to an unknown school and received a no-name degree then it really doesn't matter which comes first. Whatever you decide, it is best to consistently follow that sequence throughout your education section.

Big Name School Layout

EDUCATION **Princeton University**, Princeton, NJ
Bachelor of Arts, Sociology, May 1995

No-Name School Layout, Stress on Major

EDUCATION *Bachelor of Science*, **Mechanical Engineering**, May 1995
Donut State, Dunkinville, AK

The School Within the School

Many universities are divided into schools or colleges (College of Arts and Science, School of Management, and so forth). The question often arises: should you list the name of the particular school you attended within the university, or just name the university? The answer depends on how high the school ranks on the prestige scale. If it is nationally recognized, then definitely list it. Otherwise, you can skip it.

EDUCATION

New York University, Stern School Of Business, New York, NY
Bachelor of Science, **Finance /Accounting**, December 1995

Multiple Degrees

If you are listing more than one degree, you might want to begin with the one that is most relevant to your objective. There is no law that says you must list your degrees in chronological order. And if you hold a prior degree that you feel is completely irrelevant, you have every right to leave it out. For those of you pursuing a graduate degree, it is usually a good idea to indicate your thesis or dissertation topic, as well as a brief statement describing your research or hypothesis.

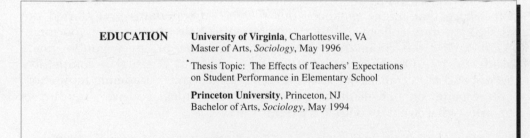

EDUCATION   **University of Virginia**, Charlottesville, VA
Master of Arts, *Sociology*, May 1996

Thesis Topic: The Effects of Teachers' Expectations on Student Performance in Elementary School

Princeton University, Princeton, NJ
Bachelor of Arts, *Sociology*, May 1994

High School

Generally it is not necessary or advisable to list your high school unless you are an underclassman. Employers are usually much more concerned about your college exploits. However, if your high school achievements are particularly impressive, or if you attended a school with a national or regional reputation, then you might want to include this information.

EDUCATION	**University of Pennsylvania**, Philadelphia, PA Bachelor of Arts, *Biology*, May 1997 **Stuyvesant High School**, New York, NY High School Diploma, May 1994 Class Rank: 5th out of 500 Student Council President

Rites of Transferring

What's most important to employers is the college from which you graduate. If you're a transfer student, only list the first college if you feel it adds something to your marketability. For example, perhaps you took classes at your first college that are relevant to your career objective, or gained valuable work experience that might enhance your resume. Or perhaps you started out at a community college and then transferred to Yale. In this case you might want to list the community college to show the progress you've made academically. On the other hand, if you started out at a highly competitive school and then transferred into a school with a weaker academic reputation, you're better off not mentioning the first school unless you want employers to ask "what went wrong?"

EDUCATION	**New York University**, New York, NY B.S., *Accounting / Actuarial Science*, May 1996 **Nassau Community College**, Garden City, NY A.A.S., *Accounting*, December 1993

Study Abroad

Increasingly, many American organizations consider it an asset for their employees to be globally minded and multilingual. They want workers who are sensitive to other cultures and adaptable to new environments.

Studying abroad or participating in an international exchange program demonstrates to employers that you are interested in expanding your world view and experience. Those of you who have participated in these activities should list them on your resume. Describe the activities you were engaged in while abroad. Were you studying the host country's language, literature, or history? Were you employed? Did you live with a local family? Did you travel extensively?

Education	**Boston University**, Boston, MA
	B.A., Political Science, May 1996
	BMT, Jerusalem, Israel
	Junior Year Abroad, 1994-1995
	Gained a deep appreciation for Israeli culture and history through a mixture of formal education and extensive travel. Spent six months living and working on a kibbutz.

Should You List Your GPA?

The answer depends on a number of factors. The first consideration is how employers in your prospective field view grades. In some fields, such as accounting, it is practically mandatory to list one's GPA. Omitting it could mean the employer will just assume it's low.

If you're pursuing a field in which grades are not a major criteria, then the question of whether or not to list your GPA depends on how good it is. Based on the responses in chapter 5, 3.3 is probably a safe cutoff. Once you've been out of school a few years the whole topic of grades will be moot anyway.

Which GPA Should You List?

List whichever GPA is the most impressive—overall, major, or minor. (By the way, it is permissible to round your GPA up to the nearest tenth of a point.) If your grades are high across the board, just list your overall average. Of course if you graduated with an extraordinary GPA, the odds are that you also received certain academic honors. If this is the case you may want to skip listing GPA, and just list your honors. Phi Beta Kappa has a much nicer ring to it than 3.8.

If You Have a Low GPA

Believe it or not, there are a couple of ways out of this predicament. The most effective method is to improve your performance in the classroom. The next best option is to consider whether your GPA has been improving steadily. For example, perhaps your grades were lousy in your freshman year but have skyrocketed since then. If this is the case, you can calculate your grades from the point at which they began to rise. On your resume this would read something like: "Achieved a 3.3 GPA over the past three semesters."

If this technique doesn't solve your problem of a low GPA, the next alternative is to review your academic record and take note of all the classes in which you received high marks. If these classes are somehow related, you could state a GPA on your resume that pertains to this area of concentration ("Achieved a GPA of 3.4 in Russian history classes"). Of course this is a bit of a stretch, and you may just be better off not mentioning your grades at all.

---

1   **EDUCATION**   **University of Virginia**, Charlottesville, VA
Bachelor of Arts, *History*, May 1996
Overall GPA: 3.4

2   **EDUCATION**   **University of Virginia**, Charlottesville, VA
Bachelor of Arts, *History*, May 1996
Major GPA: 3.7

3   **EDUCATION**   **University of Virginia**, Charlottesville, VA
Bachelor of Arts, *History*, May 1996
Overall GPA since sophomore year: 3.5

Honors and Awards

Honors and awards are an objective verification of your abilities and achievements, and thereby give you credibility. This is important because for the most part a resume is a subjective document. When an employer reads that you were honored as the top student in a course or competition, your status is immediately elevated a couple of notches. After all, you have been officially commended by a panel of experts.

When listing honors and awards, try to stress those that are most relevant to the job for which you are applying. Keep your list fairly short, and make sure you describe the honor or award if it is not self-explanatory. For example, if you received the Waldo Watson Award, no one but you will have the slightest idea what it's about unless you explain. If appropriate, try to give the reader a sense of the competitiveness of the selection process. Was it national, regional, or local? How many other students were up for consideration?

EDUCATION

New York University, New York, NY
B.S., *Accounting / Actuarial Science*, May 1996

Honors   Racoosin Scholar—participate in annual overseas excursions, attend monthly guest lectures, coordinate annual community service projects.

Dean's List (four semesters)

National Honor Society

Relevant Coursework

If academics are your strong suit, you might want to mention a few of the classes you've taken that are particularly relevant to your career objective. Prioritize your list of classes in the order of their relevance to the employer. The first class you list should be the one that really makes the employer take notice.

Stick to listing classes in which you've performed well, and that are not typical requirements for your major. For example, if you're an economics major, everyone knows that you have to take micro and macro, so why bother mentioning them? Instead, you might list the seminar you took, Economies of the Third World. You can take some creative license with the names of the classes you've taken, as the official course names at many universities often shed little light onto their content. For example, you could modify the title "Calculus III" to read "Advanced Calculus." Also, it is best to omit from your list classes in which you acquired hard skills such as programming in COBOL or speaking French, as these skills would be more appropriately listed in your "Skills" section. If you've taken intro, intermediate, and advanced courses in the same subject area, only list the advanced course as it will be assumed that you took the prerequisites. Finally, if you conducted some particularly interesting research for a class, or wrote a paper that you're really proud of, then by all means describe those projects.

---

1 | **EDUCATION** | **Lehigh University**, Bethlehem, PA
Bachelor of Arts, History, May 1995

Relevant Course Work | American Constitutional Law
United States History
Women in Law
Power & Politics in America

---

2 | **EDUCATION** | *Bachelor of Science*, **Mechanical Engineering**, May 1994
University of the Philippines, Manila

Relevant Courses | **Machine Design**
Designed rubber band powered cars capable of performing Figure 8s; constructed paper bridges strong enough to support a 25 pound weight.

Turbo Pascal
Wrote a computer program to calculate the dollar's equivalent in 15 foreign currencies.

Stating your accomplishments on your resume is fine and dandy, but the real test comes when you're asked to discuss them on an interview. Sandy Kapoor, a Senior Technical Consultant at a major financial institution, warns that "if you list a project on your resume, make sure you know extremely well what you did and why. You'll need to tell me in detail why you approached the task a certain way. It's not enough to be good with the buzzwords . . . you have to answer the why's."

EXPERIENCE

The "Experience" section is the heart and soul of your resume. This section can make or break you. Unfortunately this part is also the most difficult to write, particularly for those of you who prefer not to sing your own praises. The Experience section is a place to sing loudly about your accomplishments and achievements. Fundamentally, you are attempting to answer the employer's question: "If I hire you today, what can you do for me tomorrow?" To answer this adequately you'll need to offer concrete examples of your skills, and how you've used them to solve problems. You'll find that most employers are interested in practical solutions as opposed to theoretical speculation, unless of course they are looking to hire a theoretician.

Before you begin to write, arrange your accomplishments in the order of their relevancy to the employer. At the same time consider what you would like to be doing in the future. Stress those skills that you most want to use, and play down or omit those that you'd rather leave on the shelf.

To write your descriptions, you'll need a little help from the power verbs that were introduced in chapter 4. They can spice up your prose and give it a little bite. For example, instead of using passive constructions like "Responsibilities included selling raffle tickets," or "Duties consisted of designing logos," you could say "Sold raffle tickets" and "Designed logos." Remember to use the tense that accurately reflects when the activity took place. There is no need to use the "-ing" form of a verb when past or present tense suffices.

You'll also need a little help from our other friends, the adjectives. When possible and appropriate, try to quantify or qualify your accomplishments and responsibilities. Quantification in particular seems to work well in our numbers-oriented society. Instead of saying "Counseled students and alumni," you can say "Counseled over 1,000 students and alumni annually." Or instead of saying "Resolved customer disputes," you can say "Resolved customer disputes in a diplomatic and sensitive manner."

Keep your descriptions brief and to the point. Six lines of text is usually more than enough. There is no need to burden the reader with superfluous details. You can always explain the finer points of the job on your interview.

WHY IS THIS JOB DIFFERENT THAN ALL OTHER JOBS?

As you write the descriptions of your work experiences, consider the following five questions:

1. What Did You Accomplish or Achieve?

Employers are looking for results. They also want to get a sense of whether you take the initiative, or just do what you're told. This is the place to show that you're a go-getter. Remember to quantify or qualify whatever it is you accomplished. If you're drawing blanks, try asking yourself the following questions: What distinguishes you from your colleagues? Are you ever consistently praised by your boss for the way you perform certain tasks? Do your co-workers ask for your advice or opinion about how to carry out certain projects? Have you been designated to train new employees in certain procedures? Have you made any recommendations to your boss that have been adopted or put into use? Have any of your ideas regarding policy or procedure been implemented?

2. What Were Your Major Responsibilities?

In other words, what did you do all day long? For some reason it is easy for people to talk about their jobs, but when it comes to writing about them it's like pulling teeth. If this is true for you, then I suggest that you talk first and write later. Keep a little tape recorder handy to record your thoughts as they occur to you. Later you can translate your thoughts into prose.

As much as possible, try to indicate how well you performed your job responsibilities. If you just list the duties of your position, your description will be dull and lifeless and the reader will fall asleep. But don't take this to mean that you can indiscriminately throw adjectives and numbers all over the place. Use modifiers prudently.

3. What New Skills or Knowledge Did You Acquire?

This is particularly relevant for describing an internship or volunteer experience where you primarily played the role of apprentice. While you may not have had many major job responsibilities, you nonetheless developed new abilities, improved your skills, and learned the ins and outs of a new field. This is nothing to sneeze at. The mere fact that you received in-depth exposure to a field, and were able to interact with professionals in that field on a regular basis, is enough to make an employer take you seriously. After all, you are now familiar with the territory, the lingo, and the culture of that field.

In describing an internship or volunteer experience, you might want to mention that you attended staff meetings, observed experienced professionals at work, learned how the organization operates, became fluent in the jargon of the field, and provided administrative and technical support to staff, management, and executives. The point is to show that you have been groomed and trained to join the ranks of the professionals.

4. What Qualifies as Experience?

Just about anything can be considered experience. You can include full-time, part-time, seasonal employment, volunteer work, internships, consulting, freelancing, military service, raising children, and extracurricular activities. Just make sure that the employer understands the capacity in which you were employed. You wouldn't want someone to think that you were a full-time staff member when in fact you were volunteering five hours a week. In any case, the issue is not whether you were paid, but rather what you accomplished through your efforts.

5. Which Information Should You Include?

At the bare minimum you need to include the name of your employer, the employer's location (city and state, or country if it's overseas), your job title, dates of employment, and a description of what you achieved. You might also want to include the name of the division or department within the organization, if it's relevant, as well as a brief description of the organization. What products or services does it provide? How large is it? Is it domestic or international?

EXPERIENCE	**Associate Merchandiser**, 1993-Present Signet Sportswear, Ltd., New York, NY
	Signet is a $30 million women's sportswear manufacturer.

PRESENTATION

Although there's no doubt that employers prefer bulleted job descriptions, keep in mind that bullets generally take up quite a bit more space than paragraphs. If you do use bullets, you might want to try a theme-oriented approach in which each bullet addresses a particular skill area. For example, all of your accomplishments pertaining to customer service would be clustered together beside one bullet. Such an approach enables you to avoid listing only one accomplishment per line. It's also a good idea to leave a smidgen of space between each bulleted statement so that when viewed as a group they don't appear to be one big blob.

Basic Bulleted Description

Summers '90 & '91	**Camp Mesorah**, *Waiter/Cook*	Cleveland, OH

- Efficiently served up to four tables simultaneously.
- Prepared meals for up to 500 diners at a time.

Bullets Organized by themes

SOCIAL SERVICE EXPERIENCE

Substance Abuse Counselor / HIV Program Coordinator, 1993-Present
Lafayette Medical Management, New York, NY

- Manage a case load of 70 clients currently on methadone maintenance. Provide individual and group counseling, with a focus on issues such as goal setting, employment, education, nutrition, health care, and hygiene.

- Created the HIV Counseling Program which services over 200 participants. Coordinate weekly rap sessions, arrange guest lectures and staff training, organize various group activities, distribute condoms and safe sex literature, and conduct pre- and post-HIV test counseling. Supervise two assistants.

- Prepare monthly, quarterly, semi-annual, and annual reports based on case reviews. Monitor the results of weekly toxicological/urine profiles and take action as necessary. Conduct intake interviews with newly accepted program participants.

WHAT'S IN A TITLE?

Job titles tend to be fairly meaningless. Some give an inflated sense of the job, and others grossly underestimate it. If you feel your title doesn't do you justice, you may want to omit it or modify it slightly to make it more accurate. For example, if your official title is Grade 3 Filing Clerk, but you really do the job of an Administrative Assistant, then go ahead and call yourself an Administrative, or Office, Assistant. Just make sure you're honest with the employer if they ask for your official title on an interview or job application. For those of you who are self-employed, you can either list "self-employed" or "free-lance" for your title, or list the names of a few of your major clients. It's probably not a good idea to list yourself as the president of your company if it's a one-person outfit. Keep in mind that employers are sometimes suspect of applicants who have already gone into business for themselves. They worry that such people may be too independent-minded and will not be able to work as part of a team. To avert the employer's apprehension, you may want to tone down some of your entrepreneurial activities.

Elevator Going Up

Promotions are usually interpreted as evidence of high quality performance. You can demonstrate your promotion within an organization by creating two separate entries under a single employer heading—there's no need to list all the employer information twice. Another option is to merge the two descriptions under your current title, and to indicate at the end of the listing that you were promoted from your original position. If you were promoted more than once, or faster than is customary, this should also be indicated (e.g. "promoted twice within 9 months").

Title or Name of Organization—Which Comes First?

The answer depends on which piece of information you believe will have the greatest impact. If you worked at a well-known organization as a gopher then you're better off listing the organization first. On the other hand if you were a vice president at a small company that nobody's ever heard of, go with your title first. The annoying part is that once you've selected the sequence for your first job, you must stay consistent throughout the rest of the resume. Otherwise employers won't know which to expect first, title or organization name, and this will surely aggravate them.

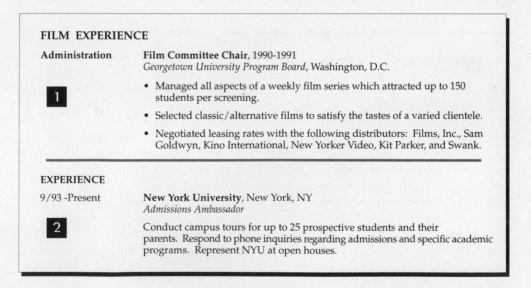

FILM EXPERIENCE

Administration

Film Committee Chair, 1990-1991
Georgetown University Program Board, Washington, D.C.

1

- Managed all aspects of a weekly film series which attracted up to 150 students per screening.

- Selected classic/alternative films to satisfy the tastes of a varied clientele.

- Negotiated leasing rates with the following distributors: Films, Inc., Sam Goldwyn, Kino International, New Yorker Video, Kit Parker, and Swank.

EXPERIENCE

9/93 -Present

New York University, New York, NY
Admissions Ambassador

2

Conduct campus tours for up to 25 prospective students and their parents. Respond to phone inquiries regarding admissions and specific academic programs. Represent NYU at open houses.

Does Anybody Really Know What Time It Is?

Listing dates of employment is a regrettable necessity unless you want to make it obvious that you're trying to hide something. At least you have some control over how conspicuously the dates appear. If your career progression has been logical and steady, and you have no major gaps in your experience, then you can list your dates of employment in a prominent location. However, if you've had a series of short-term jobs, taken time off to study in a Tibetan monastery, or have been out of the work force for a long time, your task is to bury dates so they receive as little attention as possible. Try placing them at the end of your description so they blend nicely into the rest of the text.

The Buried Date Approach

EXPERIENCE

Avon Products, Inc.   *Marketing Intern*

Provide administrative and technical support to the Planning, Analysis, and Research team. Assist with the coordination and moderation of focus groups conducted nationwide; handle logistics; collect qualitative data to be used in forecasting. Contributed to the development of a database designed to store information collected during quantitative and qualitative clinics. Maintain database, clean data, and classify information to be entered. 1994-Present

Covering Up Gaps

Although it is quite common to list the month and year of one's employment start and end dates, at times it is more advantageous to list only the year. For the sake of argument let's say that you started working at Taco Bell in June of 1993 and left your job in February of 1994. Five months later you started a new job at the Gap where you are presently employed. By using the "year only method" the employer will have no idea that there was a five month gap. On your resume it will appear as though you were employed continuously from 1993 through the present. Of course, if you're asked about specific dates you should always be honest.

How Far Back and How Much?

Recent experience carries the most weight, but if there's something you've done in your past that you feel warrants mentioning, then by all means mention it. How many jobs should you list? That depends largely on the length of your job descriptions and the amount of information in your other categories. Assuming an average-length description, you probably won't be able to fit more than four to five jobs on a one-page resume, so be selective.

If you held a variety of odd jobs throughout college that don't require individual descriptions, you could lump them all together under one heading such as "Additional Experience." At least in this way you are demonstrating to the employer that you have worked steadily while going to school, and have been exposed to a wide range of experiences. You also are conveying a positive impression about your work ethic.

ADDITIONAL EXPERIENCE

1993-Present   Worked an average of 20 hours per week while attendingclasses full-time. Held a variety of positions, including waitress, word processor, caterer, and entertainer at children's parties.

TWO-PAGE RESUMES

If you absolutely must go to a two-page resume, make sure your name appears in the upper right corner of the second page, in case the two pages are separated. A debate still rages about whether the pages should be stapled. If they are, just pray the employer doesn't cut herself on the staple. The fact is, though, that you really don't need a two-page resume unless you have a tremendous amount of experience, say ten years' worth, or are seeking a position in academia or non-profit where more detailed job descriptions are the norm. Your resume might also require a second page to accommodate lists of publications, presentations, and research projects.

WHAT TO CALL YOUR EXPERIENCE SECTION

If your Experience section will be comprised of both paid and non-paid positions, then you might as well just call it "Experience." On the other hand, if it consists entirely of paid employment, then you have the option of calling it "Professional Experience." You could also label your Experience section by using the name of the skill or field being stressed as the main heading ("Marketing Experience," or "Photography Experience"). Another possibility is to split your experience into two broad categories such as "Related Experience" and "Additional Experience." Whichever approach you choose is fine as long as it's founded on good, solid marketing logic.

WHAT IF I HAVE NO EXPERIENCE?

Not to worry. Well, at least don't panic. Remember that internships, volunteer work, and extracurricular activities are all fair game for the Experience section. If you haven't been active in any of these three areas, you'll need to place a lot of emphasis on your Education section. That's fine as long as you've performed well academically and engaged in some interesting class projects. Realistically, though, even if you're a straight-A student, it behooves you to start getting involved outside of the ivory tower if you hope to be able to compete for jobs with your peers.

ACTIVITIES

For all of you current students and recent graduates, here's your chance to show the prospective employer that college is about more than just books and beer. This is an opportunity to demonstrate that you've had a well-rounded college experience, enhanced by involvement in a variety of school and community clubs, organizations, and athletics. By mentioning your extracurriculars, you are attempting to convey that you have developed certain abilities and personal qualities that will make you an asset to any organization.

If you've been heavily involved in extracurriculars, but have had limited professional experience, you might want to bump your activities section ahead of your experience section. If your involvement has been moderate to light, it might make more sense to incorporate your activities into either your Education or Experience sections.

If you choose to create a separate Activities section, then you should describe each activity just as you would a job. Focus on accomplishments, results, and the development of new skills. List the name of the club or organization in which you participated, along with your title or affiliation. Dates are really not necessary for activities and only serve to clutter up your resume. If you've held elected office, make sure to mention this. Getting elected implies you've been able to elicit the support and confidence of others—not an easy feat. Also note whether you've received any honors, awards, or official commendation as a result of your extracurricular involvement.

Your first step in designing the Activities section is to create a prioritized list of all your activities. Begin with those that would be of greatest relevance to your target employer. Positions where you displayed leadership or had significant responsibility should come first (for example, treasurer, president, or founder of an organization). Also high on your list should be any involvement you had in activities related to your target field. For example, if you're interested in becoming a buyer at a department store, then it would be a good idea to stress the student fashion show you organized last year.

Some employers consider service-oriented activities extremely important, as they indicate that your heart is in the right place. Another winner is involvement in varsity athletics. Many interviewers, especially men, love to chat about sports, and most have a good sense of the commitment, discipline, and drive required to compete at the college level. Lower on your list would come basic club memberships, particularly if you weren't a very active member. Never list an affiliation if you weren't genuinely involved with the organization. Many people do this because they think it "looks good," but imagine how bad it will look on the interview when the recruiter grills you about a club in which you never actually participated.

There is some debate as to how employers perceive fraternities and sororities. This probably has a great deal to do with whether the employer was ever involved in a fraternity or sorority, and if so, whether or not they had a positive experience. Their view may also be contingent on the reputation of the particular fraternity or sorority in question. In any case, it is rather unlikely that the employer will hold anything against you just because you were involved with one of these organizations. And if by some stroke of luck the person interviewing you happens to be a brother or sister, then you could have clear sailing. At the very least you'll certainly have something to talk about.

ACTIVITIES	**Connections**, Alumni Mentor Program, *Mentee* • Meet regularly with an alumnus to discuss academic, career, and business issues.
1	**Society for Creative Anachronism**, *Treasurer* • Oversaw the club's annual budget of $5,000. **Science Fiction Club**, *Vice President* • Coordinate the publication of the club's annual magazine.
Activities	Junior Varsity Basketball Team, Point Guard
2	Upward Bound Program, Tutor Kappa Delta Rho, Fraternity Member Economics Club, Member

SKILLS

Employers will scan this section to see if you possess any "hard" skills that could come in handy. These include: speaking a foreign language; programming a computer; utilizing various software packages; operating a video camera, and so on. Even if you've already mentioned some of these skills in your position descriptions, the Skills section offers a nice neat summary where an employer can see the whole picture at a glance. List your skills in order of their relevancy to your target employer. If a skill has no relevancy, leave it out. Would a local accounting firm really jump for joy because you speak Punjabi?

A WORD ABOUT COMPUTER SKILLS

If you're a programmer, systems analyst, or a technically-inclined person you may want to create a special category called "Computer Skills." Depending on your target audience, you may even want to start your resume with this section. To make matters easier for the reader it's a good idea to further categorize your skills according to subheadings such as "Hardware," "Software," and "Programming Languages." Also, try to be as specific as possible. Instead of just listing the skill "word processing," list the names of the applications with which you are familiar. If you're uncertain about your level of proficiency then precede the skill with the phrase "exposure to" or "basic knowledge of." In this way you'll be covering your behind in case someone wants to give you a technical exam, which is not unusual.

A WORD ABOUT LANGUAGE SKILLS

For all you United Nations types, foreign language skills are of primary importance. They can be crucial to obtaining interviews with international organizations, and often deserve a category of their own: "Language Skills." The important thing is to qualify your level of language proficiency. Do you have speaking, reading, or writing ability? And if so, are you a beginner, intermediate, or advanced practitioner? Or better yet, are you fluent? By qualifying your skill level you can avoid the embarrassment that will surely come when an interviewer just assumes your ability is a few notches above its actual state. Trust us, it's no fun when the interviewer starts speaking to you in rapid fire Spanish, and the only reply you can humbly manage is "hasta la vista, baby."

1	**SKILLS**	Familiar with Microsoft Word and WordPerfect Conversational Italian

2	**COMPUTER SKILLS** *Languages* *Software* *Hardware*	 C, Turbo Pascal Lotus 123, Quattro Pro, Filemaker, Pagemaker, Harvard Graphics IBM PC/XT/AT/386, Macintosh

3	**LANGUAGES**	Fluent in English, French, and Portuguese Strong knowledge of Italian Understanding of written and spoken Spanish

INTERESTS

The debate continues as to whether this section should even be included on a resume. Some employers like it because it gives them a glimpse into your personality and arms them with conversational icebreakers for the interview. Don't be surprised if many of your interviews begin with questions about your interests. Other employers dismiss the Interests section as irrelevant and a waste of space. But most everyone seems to agree that if you do decide to include an interests section, the items you list should be either relevant to your career goal or fairly unique. If you're applying for a position with the Foreign Policy Association, listing international travel (and perhaps naming some of the countries or continents you've visited) makes perfect sense since presumably through your travel you've developed a greater awareness of what's going on in the world around you. It's doubtful, however, that the folks at the Foreign Policy Association could really give two tamales that you enjoy listening to New Age music.

Listing unique interests is another way to get the attention of the employer. Just be careful that whatever you list doesn't reflect negatively on your ability to make sound judgments. If you list skydiving and bungee jumping as your interests you will definitely get noticed, but few employers will consider you seriously. First of all they'll think you're a lunatic, and secondly they'll be afraid that after a couple weeks on the job you'll get injured and go on permanent disability.

If you choose to list interests simply because you want to present a side of yourself that doesn't emerge through your professional or academic life, that's okay too. Just be as specific as possible—the more generic the interest, the less interesting you will appear. For example you might want to list "mystery novels" instead of "reading," "tango" instead of "dance," "Truffaut

films" instead of "cinema," and "long distance running" instead of "fitness."
Whatever you do, don't list an interest which doesn't really arouse your
passion. With your luck that will be the one interest that the recruiter asks
about.

Also, if you've competed successfully in one or more of your areas of
interest, you might want to mention this. Just be careful not to give the
impression that you live and die for your interests—remember that you're
applying for a job. A final word of caution: stay away from topics like religion
and politics unless you desire to be labeled according to your beliefs.

The fun part about including interests on your resume is that their effect
on the reader is completely unpredictable. Some interviewers will want to
chat with you for hours because you both like to ski at Stowe. Others will
gloss over the section and basically ignore it. Still others will despise you
sight-unseen because you've indicated that you run marathons when they're
still struggling to make it once around the block.

INTERESTS	International travel (Central America, South America, and Asia), playing flute, African history, and Spanish literature.

WHAT *NOT* TO INCLUDE ON YOUR RESUME

Don't list height and weight, references, race, ethnicity, political affiliation,
marital status, the names and ages of your children, and the reasons why
you left each job. And don't staple a photo of yourself to your resume.

ADDITIONAL CATEGORIES

Well folks, that just about does it for your basic All-American resume. Now for those of you who want to get really fancy or have special career needs, you may want to consider some of the optional categories listed below.

Community Service

If you're leaning toward a career in non-profit or social service, and even if you're not, you can create a Community Service category to serve as home for all the wonderful volunteer work you've done which wasn't substantial enough to make it into your Experience section. Here you can mention the fact that every Thanksgiving you help prepare a feast at the local soup kitchen, and that each Spring you assist with coordinating the annual AIDS walk. If nothing else, listing these activities will show that you have a kind heart.

COMMUNITY SERVICE

- Burden Center for the Aging, Participant in the Friendly Visitor Program
- New York City School Volunteer Program, Tutor

Professional Affiliations or Memberships

This category is generally most appropriate for graduates who have already established themselves professionally and are active members of one or more professional associations (such as the American Psychological Association). "Active" is the key word here, meaning that you attend conferences, workshops, and seminars, and possibly serve on one of the organization's committees. Including this category demonstrates that you are committed to your field, and are interested in developing yourself professionally.

Professional Affiliations

American Association for Counseling and Development
Career Development Specialists' Network
Career Resource Mangers' Association

Professional Development or Continuing Education

This is a perfect section in which to list all the workshops, seminars, and classes you've attended that were not part of your formal degree program. If you were employed at a large organization, perhaps you took advantage of training that was offered in areas like conflict resolution, creative problem solving, or crisis management. Or maybe you sought out adult education classes on your own to keep abreast of what's going on in your field. The point is that you have taken the initiative to enrich yourself, acquire new skills, and build your knowledge base. Those are achievements worth mentioning.

When listing continuing education classes, the main concern is to indicate the subject being studied. When you took the class and where is less important. However, if the course was offered by a world-renowned expert, or at a well-known institution, then feel free to list this information.

Professional Development
A Neurodevelopmental Approach to Baby Treatment—5-day course
Neurodevelopmental Treatment of Children with Cerebral Palsy—8-week course
Alternate Systems of Communication for the Person with Neuromuscular Disorders

---

Licenses/Certifications

This information is essential for nurses, social workers, real estate brokers, stock brokers, guidance counselors, teachers, and a host of other professionals whose fields are governed by a licenser.

Licenses/Certificates
New York Gaming School, Certificate of Completion, 1980
New Jersey Gaming Commission, Key Casino Employee, 1980-Present

---

Publications

If you're going after a job in academia, journalism, or publishing, it's a good idea to list publications where your work has appeared. Be selective. You can always submit a complete list at the interview. Make sure to include the names of any co-authors, the title of the article or book, the name of the publication, the name and location of the publisher (for books only), and the date of publication.

SELECTED PUBLICATIONS

"Literature Adds Up," a chapter within the book *Fact or Fiction: Reading and Writing Across the Curriculum*, The International Reading Association, 1992.

"Falling in Love with the Subject: Romance in Education," *The Holistic Education Review*, Spring 1991.

"Incorporating Video into the Curriculum: A Teacher's Perspective," *Video and Learning Newsletter*, Winter/Spring 1993.

Exhibitions

This category is for fine artists, commercial artists, and craftspeople who have shown work at galleries, festivals, museums, and other exhibition spaces. As with everything else on your resume, lead with your strengths and be selective. You don't have to list your entire exhibition record, just the highlights. Start off with your most impressive solo exhibitions and work back through your group exhibitions. Make sure you list the name and location of the exhibition space. You may also want to list the title of the show, the medium of the work (especially if you work in more than one), and the year of the show. Also indicate under a separate subheading whether any of your work has been purchased for the permanent collection of a museum or private collector.

SOLO EXHIBITIONS

1993	Crawford and Sloan Gallery, New York, NY "Romantic Visions"
1992	Fotozeller, Berlin, Germany "Peace on Mars"

Military Service

Contrary to popular belief, an employer rarely views military service as a negative. Most people seem to recognize that being in the military has its positive aspects, and if they don't get it, it's your job to persuade them. Talk about your abilities as a leader and decision maker, and stress your drive, determination, self-discipline, and team orientation. If you served as an officer, indicate your most significant accomplishments and responsibilities on your resume.

MILITARY SERVICE

1980-1984   Achieved the rank of Captain in the Israeli Army
                                 • Oversaw 50 soldiers and 5 officers.

Visa, Visa, Who's Got the Visa?

If you're an international student hoping to work for an American company in the United States, you face a special challenge. You have to convince employers to hire you instead of an American, even though there's a chance you may not remain permanently in this country. That's a big risk for the employer, considering the amount of time and money they're going to invest to train you. Although this is no easy hurdle to overcome, it can be done. The first thing to do is sit down with your international student advisor and get all the facts about your eligibility for employment. Then you can devise a plan of action.

One approach is to not bring attention to the fact that you're an international student, in order to make employers more receptive to your initial application. The problem with this strategy is that once you're on the interview, at some point or other, you will need to disclose your international student status. This could have an adverse effect on your candidacy, as the employer may wonder why you didn't reveal this fact from the beginning.

A second approach is to be very direct, and in your initial communication make the employer aware of the fact that you are authorized to work in the United States. If you have a green card (permanent residency), or hold a visa which allows you to apply for practical training, this information can be provided at the bottom of your resume. This approach should help to allay any fears the employer might have about the status of your work eligibility.

It may, however, hurt your chances of obtaining an interview with employers who have a predisposition not to hire international students.

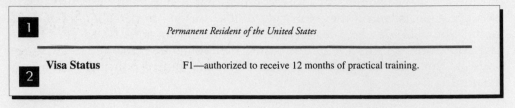

1 *Permanent Resident of the United States*

2 **Visa Status** F1—authorized to receive 12 months of practical training.

IN CONCLUSION

You made it through the mother of all resume writing chapters. You should now have in your hand a nearly finished draft of your resume. Pretty exciting, huh? In the next chapter we're going to learn how to make that resume look simply gorgeous.

CHAPTER 7

RESUME DESIGN 101

YOUR RESUME'S GOT TO LOOK SHARP

To paraphrase Vidal Sasoon, "If your resume doesn't look good, then you don't look good." A poorly presented resume is likely to kill any chance you may have had of obtaining a job interview, regardless of your qualifications. Most unattractive resumes spend only a few seconds in an employer's hand before they are condemned to the trash can. If the resume is lucky it will be reincarnated via the recycling bin. If not, it will end up in some garbage dump buried under twenty tons of non-biodegradable waste.

> ### LOOKS COUNT
>
> "The way your resume looks is extremely important. It's going to reach the recruiter in a pile with fifty other resumes. If your resume doesn't look inviting it won't get read, even if you have the best qualifications."
>
> —Linda Gaglio, University Relations Manager, Chase Manhattan Bank, N.A.

The point is that you've got to look sharp on paper in order to make the first cut in the employment screening process. The employers we surveyed cited readability and presentation as the two qualities they most value in a resume. This means that no matter how outstanding your credentials, if your resume is sloppy, disorganized, or just plain ugly, you stand a good chance of receiving a rejection notice. Employers reason that if you can't take the time and care necessary to present yourself professionally on paper, then what guarantee do they have that you'll act like a professional on the job? The doubts will begin to slowly creep into their heads. Will you dress appropriately? How will you behave with clients? Will you use sound judgment in emergency situations? How well will you get along with your colleagues? Do you have a chip on your shoulder?

Good News for the Non-Artist

Fortunately, designing an attractive, readable resume is not a task of Herculean proportions. Rest assured that to pull this off you need not be artistically inclined—good common sense will do just fine. Once you understand the basic layout and design principles, you can't go wrong. And for those of you who would rather take the easy way out, we've provided nine time-tested, time-saving templates.

Production and Design Tools

Before we go any further, you'll need to have the following at your fingertips: a draft of your resume, a computer equipped with word processing software, several sheets of 8 1/2 x 11 paper, and a printer. We'll discuss printing and paper in the next chapter, but for now let's turn our attention briefly to computers and software.

Please say "yes, I am proficient in one or more word processing packages." If word processing is not currently one of the skills in your repertoire, then you should put this book down and go sign up for a word processing class. Better yet, take a friend to dinner and have her teach you. The fact is that practically no matter what job you apply for, word processing will be a basic requirement.

Whether you use an IBM, PC clone, or Macintosh computer is not really an issue. Nor is it crucial which word processing package you use, so long as it has good flexibility, offers an array of typefaces (also known as fonts), and is likely to be on the market for a while. In the end, the deciding factors will probably be cost and convenience. What we can't recommend at this point, however, are any of the resume-writing software packages. They just don't seem to make the process that much easier, and more importantly, they don't offer the kind of flexibility you'll need to design a first-rate resume.

COMMENCING YOUR MASTERPIECE

Take a seat at your computer and switch it on. Insert your disk, and you're ready to rock. Remember to always save your work on your own disk, especially if you're doing your resume in a computer lab. If you've only saved on the hard drive, there's a good chance that by the next day all your work will have been deleted from the system. Create a new document and name it. If you anticipate putting together more than one version of your resume, make sure that your document names are indicative of their contents or you'll be wasting valuable time trying to figure out which document is which.

MARGINALLY SPEAKING

The first thing you're going to do is set your margins. They serve two important functions. First, they act like a frame, providing a welcome border of white space around your text; and second, they serve as a built-in memo pad for employers, many of whom like to make notes directly on your resume. To play it safe set your margins at one inch on all four sides. If you need extra space they can always be decreased later to a minimum of .5 inches, or if your resume is a bit on the skimpy side, they can be widened to a maximum of 1.5 inches. For the sake of balance, try to keep your margins approximately the same on all four sides.

FONT-O-RAMA

Your next step is to select a typeface, of which there are two basic kinds—serif and sans serif—with thousands of variations of each. A serif typeface such as Palatino or Times is characterized by letters that have small finishing strokes, affectionately referred to by the non-design crowd as "curlicues." In contrast, the letters of a sans-serif typeface, such as Avant Garde or Geneva, have no such finishing strokes. Most graphic designers agree that serif typefaces are preferred for large blocks of text, while sans serif typefaces are more effective for short passages, headlines, and captions. It is best to stick with one typeface on a resume. Some of the more popular typefaces that are suitable for resumes are illustrated below:

TIMES

EDUCATION   **Northwestern University**, Evanston, IL
B.A., *English*, May 1995

NEW CENTURY SCHOOLBOOK

EDUCATION   **Northwestern University**, Evanston, IL
B.A., *English*, May 1995

PALATINO

EDUCATION   **Northwestern University**, Evanston, IL
B.A., *English*, May 1995

BOOKMAN

EDUCATION   **Northwestern University**, Evanston, IL
B.A., *English*, May 1995

There are three main factors you need to consider in choosing a typeface: readability, attractiveness, and appropriateness. Are the letters and words easy to distinguish? Do most people find the typeface pleasing to the eye? Does it convey an image of professionalism? Remember, you are not printing an invitation to a wedding or Halloween party. Make sure to get the opinion of someone whose eye you trust before printing the final version of your resume. If in doubt, you can always fall back on the old reliable Times, the most popular resume typeface in America.

Size Counts

Now that you've selected a typeface you'll need to pick a type size for the body of your text. Type size is also referred to as point size (72 points = 1 inch). Depending on the typeface being used, you will probably want to go with a point size between 10 and 12. The only way to figure out what size to use is to print a few lines and see how it looks. If you have to squint, go up a point or two. If it looks like a children's book, bring it down a point or two. When looking at the following examples, keep in mind that the page size of this book is much smaller than your 8.5" x 11" resume, so the 12-point size may look too big here, but it won't on your resume.

---

1 TOO BIG—Times, 14 PT

EDUCATION **Northwestern University**, Evanston, IL
B.A., *English*, May 1995

---

2 JUST RIGHT—Times, 12 PT

EDUCATION **Northwestern University**, Evanston, IL
B.A., *English*, May 1995

---

3 SMALL BUT ACCEPTABLE—Times, 10 PT

EDUCATION **Northwestern University**, Evanston, IL
B.A., *English*, May 1995

---

4 TOO SMALL—Times, 8 PT

EDUCATION **Northwestern University**, Evanston, IL
B.A., *English*, May 1995

For most resumes you'll want to use three different type sizes—one for the basic text, one for the category headings, and one for your name. The headings should be about one to two points larger than the main text, and your name should be about two to four points larger than the headings. If you want to get fancy with your name, try making the first letter of your first and last names another two to four points larger than the rest of the letters in your name, like so:

Timothy Haft

LAYOUT 101

There are two basic approaches to laying out and designing a resume. Our preference is to type all the information first, flush left, then choose a layout after we get a sense of the quantity of information with which we're dealing. The other approach is to decide on a layout right out of the starting gate, and then pray that it works. Often it does, but sometimes you have either too little or too much text for the layout you've selected, leaving you in the unenviable position of either having to edit out information, add blank spaces, change your margins, or alter the layout entirely.

Your next set of layout decisions has to do with where to place the different elements of your resume. As you know, your name, address and phone number will go on top. Most people center their name with the address and phone number below, but if you're running out of space, you may want to string all the information across the top of your resume like a letterhead.

Since the eye reads from left to right, it is usually advisable to place your category headings on the far left where they will be readily noticed. This is crucial because the headings serve as a guide for the employer, allowing them to efficiently scan your resume. The descriptions which pertain to each category should either be indented below the main heading, or listed parallel to it.

Parallel Listing (Tab set at 2")

EXPERIENCE

9/93-Present

New York University, New York, NY
Admissions Ambassador

Conduct campus tours for up to 25 prospective students and their parents. Respond to phone inquiries regarding admissions and specific academic programs. Represent NYU at open houses.

Indented Listing (Tab set at .5")

EXPERIENCE

Avon Products, Inc.   *Marketing Intern*

Provide administrative and technical support to the Planning, Analysis, and Research team. Assist with the coordination and moderation of focus groups conducted nationwide; handle logistics, collect qualitative data to be used in forecasting. 1993-Present.

Once you've got your headings in place, you'll need to decide where to place the supporting information. If you're setting up a parallel listing, indenting somewhere between 1.5 inches and 2.25 inches is usually fine, depending on the typeface you're using. If you're indenting below the category heading, shoot for about .5 inches to 1 inch depending on how much text you're trying to squeeze on the page.

The possibilities for arranging items such as employer name and location, job title, and dates of employment are endless, but suffice it to say that whatever you believe to be your strongest selling point should be placed in the most prominent spot. This should either be your title or the name of your employer. Depending on how conspicuous you want them to be, dates can either be placed to the far left or right, immediately after your job title, or at the end of your job description. Employer location, which is probably the least significant piece of data, can either be placed wide to the right, after the name of your employer, or omitted altogether. Check out the samples in the next chapter to get a look at different variations.

IS YOUR RESUME SPACED OUT?

Now that all of your qualifications have found a home, give your resume the once over and look at the spacing. Is it too cluttered? Are there gaping holes of white space big enough to drive a truck through? Is it obvious where one category ends and another begins?

Blank space is crucial if the reader is going to be able to make sense of your resume. The greatest amount of space should come between major categories. There should also be a reasonable space between the end of one job and the beginning of the next. Leave a smaller space between your employer information and the beginning of your job description, as well as between each bulleted accomplishment statement.

Graphically Speaking

Okay, we're almost in the home stretch. Now it's time to add some finishing touches. There are four main techniques to consider: **bolding**, CAPITAL-IZING, • bulleting (you can substitute dashes, diamonds, boxes, arrows, checks, pointing hands, or asterisks for bullets), and *italicizing*. All of these will add distinction and emphasis to your text in varying degrees. Underlining, which was once popular, is not recommended because it looks sloppy, and has a nasty habit of slicing through the lower half of g's, q's, p's, y's and j's. Capitals take up a lot of space and should be used sparingly. Bullets work best for highlighting individual accomplishments. Bold print is most appropriate for category headings and other information that requires major emphasis. Italics lend a softer touch, and are effective for highlighting key information.

Whichever graphic devices you use, make sure that your design style is consistent. If you italicize your first job title, then every job title on your resume should be italicized. Don't suddenly switch to another technique. You will confuse the reader. Also be careful not to use the same graphic technique for adjacent items. For example, if you bold both your job title and the name of your employer, neither item will stand out. Highlighting key words within the body of your text is not recommended. Usually the reader can figure out for themselves what's important in a sentence.

We also take a rather conservative view when it comes to adding symbols and pictures to resumes. First of all, only do this if you're applying for a creative position such as art director or graphic designer. If done well, these additions can spice up your resume and help it stand out from the crowd. If done poorly, which they usually are, they make your resume look "cutesy" and unprofessional while wasting valuable space. Remember, no one is hiring you to be cute—they're hiring you to get a job done.

About the Templates

The layout templates that follow have been designed to make life a little easier for you. All the information regarding format, typeface, type size, and tab stops has been provided. For ease of presentation certain assumptions have been made regarding the categories to be included, as well as their sequence. Feel free to make modifications as you see fit.

Also, because employers vary in terms of their preference for different resume styles, each template has been rated as follows: 1=traditional, 2=moderate, and 3=artistic. The traditional styles are best for conservative fields such as accounting and banking. Moderate styles are appropriate for most fields, with the exception of those just cited. The artistic styles are best when applying for creative or artistic positions.

NAME

Address
Address
Telephone Number

EXPERIENCE

Title, Dates

Employer, Location
Description
Description
Description

Title, Dates

Employer, Location
Description
Description
Description '

Title, Dates

Employer, Location
Description
Description
Description

Title, Dates

Employer, Location
Description
Description
Description

EDUCATION

Degree, Date

School, Location

SKILLS

Skills
Skills
Skills

Hollywood

Format:	Reverse Chronological
Rating:	3
Typeface:	Bookman
Type Size:	Name: 18 pt.
	Headings: 11 pt.
	Text: 10 pt.
	Tabs: 3"

NAME
Address
Address
Telephone Number

— · — · — · — · — · — · — · — · — · — · — · —

PROFILE   Text
                     Text

EDUCATION   **Degree**, Date
                     School, Location

EXPERIENCE   **Employer**, Location
                     Title
                     Dates

                     Description

                     Description

                     Description

                     Employer, Location
                     Title
                     Dates

                     Description

                     Description

                     Description

                     Employer, Location
                     Title
                     Dates

                     Description

                     Description

                     Description

ACTIVITIES   Activity
                     Activity
                     Activity

SKILLS   Skills

Jersey Jammer

Format:	Reverse Chronological
Rating:	1
Typeface:	Times
Type Size:	Name: 13 pt.
	Headings: 12 pt.
	Text: 12 pt.
	Tabs: 1.75"

NAME
Address
Address
Telephone Number

SKILL HEADING

- Accomplishment
- Accomplishment
- Accomplishment
- Accomplishment

SKILL HEADING

- Accomplishment
- Accomplishment
- Accomplishment
- Accomplishment

SKILL HEADING

- Accomplishment
- Accomplishment
- Accomplishment
- Accomplishment

EMPLOYMENT HISTORY

Dates	Title, Employer, Location
Dates	Title, Employer, Location
Dates	Title, Employer, Location

EDUCATION

Degree, Date • School, Location, State College, PA

Nittany Lion	
Format:	Skills-Based
Rating:	2
Typeface:	New Century Schoolbook
Type Size:	Name: 14 pt. Headings: 12 pt. Text: 10 pt. Tab: 1.25" and 1.5"

NAME

Address • Address • Telephone Number

PROFILE

Text
Text
Text

EXPERIENCE

Employer   *Title*

Description
Description
Description
Dates

Employer   *Title*

Description
Description
Description
Dates

Employer   *Title*

Description
Description
Description
Dates

EDUCATION

School, Location
Degree, Date

Honors: Honor
                 Honor
                 Honor

SKILLS

Skills

Orange Madness

Format:	Reverse Chronological
Rating:	1
Typeface:	Palatino
Type Size:	Name: 16 pt. Headings: 12 pt. Text: 11 pt. Tabs: .5", 1.25", and 3.5"

NAME

Local Address
Address
Address
Telephone Number

Permanent Address
Address
Address
Telephone Number

OBJECTIVE

Objective

EDUCATION

School, Location
Degree, Date

Relevant Courses:

Course

Course

Course

EXPERIENCE

Dates

Employer, Title

- Accomplishment
- Accomplishment
- Accomplishment

Dates

Employer, Title

- Accomplishment
- Accomplishment
- Accomplishment

Dates

Employer, Title

- Accomplishment
- Accomplishment
- Accomplishment

ACTIVITIES

- Activity
- Activity
- Activity

SKILLS

Skills

Staten Island Special

Format:	Reverse Chronological
Rating:	2
Typeface:	New York
Type Size:	Name: 12 pt.
	Headings: 10 pt.
	Text: 10 pt.
	Tabs: 1.5" and

NAME

Address
Address
Telephone Number

EDUCATION

School, Location
Degree, Date

GPA

Honors:

- Honor
- Honor
- Honor

EXPERIENCE

Dates

Employer, Location
Title

- Accomplishment
- Accomplishment
- Accomplishment

Dates

Employer, Location
Title

- Accomplishment
- Accomplishment
- Accomplishment

ACTIVITIES

- Activity
- Activity

SKILLS

- Skills

The Black Streak

Format:	Reverse Chronological
Rating:	2
Typeface:	Palatino
Type Size:	Name: 14 pt. Headings: 12 pt. Text: 10 pt. Tabs: 1.5″ and 1.75″

NAME
Address
Address
Telephone Number

EXPERIENCE

Dates   **Employer**, Location
Title
- Accomplishment
- Accomplishment
- Accomplishment

Dates   **Employer**, Location
Title
- Accomplishment
- Accomplishment
- Accomplishment

Dates   **Employer**, Location
Title
- Accomplishment
- Accomplishment
- Accomplishment

Dates   **Employer**, Location
Title
- Accomplishment
- Accomplishment
- Accomplishment

EDUCATION   **School**, Location
Degree, Date

Honors: Honors

Activities   Activities
Activities

SKILLS   Skills

The Bostonian	
Format:	Reverse Chronological
Rating:	1
Typeface:	Helvetica
Type Size:	Name: 14 pt. Headings: 12 pt. Text: 10 pt. Tabs: 1.75" and 2"

NAME

Address • Address • Telephone Number

SUMMARY

Summary
Summary
Summary

EDUCATION

School, Location
Degree, Date

EXPERIENCE

TITLE, Organization, Location   Dates

Skill Subheading

Description
Description

Skill Subheading

Description
Description

TITLE, Organization, Location   Dates

Skill Subheading

Description
Description

Skill Subheading

Description
Description

SKILLS

Skills
Skills

The Terrapin	
Format:	Reverse Chronological
Rating:	2
Typeface:	Palatino
Type Size:	Name: 18 pt. Headings: 12 pt. Subheadings and Text: 10 pt. Tabs: .5", .63", and 5"

NAME
Address
Address
Phone

SKILL HEADING

Employer

Description
Description

Employer

Description
Description

SKILL HEADING

Employer

Description
Description

Employer

Description
Description

EDUCATION

Degree, Date • *School*, Location

PROFESSIONAL HISTORY

Employer, Title, Dates
Employer, Title, Dates
Employer, Title, Dates
Employer, Title, Dates

Woodstock	
Format:	Skills-Based
Rating:	3
Typeface:	Bookman
Type Size:	Name: 14 pt.
	Headings: 13 pt.
	Text: 12 pt.
	Tab: .5"

CHAPTER 8

SAMPLE RESUMES

The following resumes have been adapted from those of actual current college students and recent graduates. They have been selected for their overall quality and proven ability to generate job interviews. Every attempt has been made to represent a highly diversified cross-section of the population. To make life a little easier for you, we have categorized each sample resume in the following ways:

1. by the major of the candidate;
2. by the field the candidate desires to enter;
3. by the experience level of the candidate (for example, college senior with limited relevant experience).

Check the following resume guide to find the resumes that will best meet your needs.

Experience Level	Page

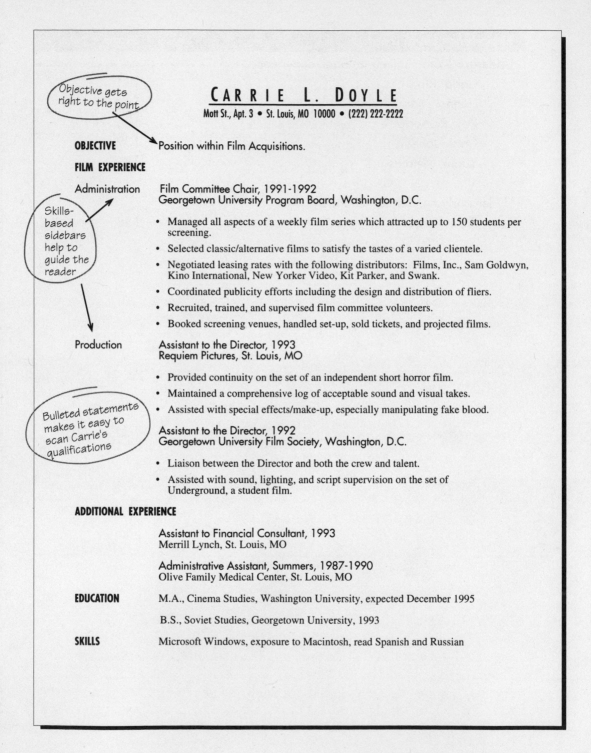

Objective gets right to the point

CARRIE L. DOYLE
Mott St., Apt. 3 • St. Louis, MO 10000 • (222) 222-2222

OBJECTIVE Position within Film Acquisitions.

FILM EXPERIENCE

Administration

Skills-based sidebars help to guide the reader

Film Committee Chair, 1991-1992
Georgetown University Program Board, Washington, D.C.

- Managed all aspects of a weekly film series which attracted up to 150 students per screening.
- Selected classic/alternative films to satisfy the tastes of a varied clientele.
- Negotiated leasing rates with the following distributors: Films, Inc., Sam Goldwyn, Kino International, New Yorker Video, Kit Parker, and Swank.
- Coordinated publicity efforts including the design and distribution of fliers.
- Recruited, trained, and supervised film committee volunteers.
- Booked screening venues, handled set-up, sold tickets, and projected films.

Production

Assistant to the Director, 1993
Requiem Pictures, St. Louis, MO

- Provided continuity on the set of an independent short horror film.
- Maintained a comprehensive log of acceptable sound and visual takes.
- Assisted with special effects/make-up, especially manipulating fake blood.

Bulleted statements makes it easy to scan Carrie's qualifications

Assistant to the Director, 1992
Georgetown University Film Society, Washington, D.C.

- Liaison between the Director and both the crew and talent.
- Assisted with sound, lighting, and script supervision on the set of Underground, a student film.

ADDITIONAL EXPERIENCE

Assistant to Financial Consultant, 1993
Merrill Lynch, St. Louis, MO

Administrative Assistant, Summers, 1987-1990
Olive Family Medical Center, St. Louis, MO

EDUCATION M.A., Cinema Studies, Washington University, expected December 1995

B.S., Soviet Studies, Georgetown University, 1993

SKILLS Microsoft Windows, exposure to Macintosh, read Spanish and Russian

ASHLYN QUEEN

777 Almost Blue Street, Apt. A • Columbus, OH 10000 • 222.555.5555

(handwritten note: Profile offers a solid overview of Ashlyn's backgound)

PROFILE

Proven ability in higher education administration with expertise in academic advisement, career counseling, and student activities. Completing M.A. in Counseling, Summer 1995. Background in marketing and management.

HIGHER EDUCATION EXPERIENCE

(handwritten note: One set of dates covers her experience at Ohio State—this avoids cluttering the resume)

Ohio State University, Columbus, OH   1994-Present

Academic/Career Advisor, College of Arts and Science

Advised undergraduate students regarding their academic and career plans, including resume preparation and interviewing skills. Redesigned Alumni Mentor Program; matched students with mentors. Designed and implemented career planning workshops.

Freshman Orientation Advisor, College of Arts and Science

Provided individual and group academic advisement to entering freshmen. Oriented students to campus and city life. Facilitated group social activities.

Pre-Registration Assistant, School of Continuing Education

Evaluated the academic and career needs of prospective students and referred them to appropriate academic departments for advisement. Maintained career library.

Community Service Center Coordinator, Office of Student Activities

Advised students and clubs regarding community service opportunities. Developed relations with community service agencies. Coordinated Hunger Clean-Up projects, and a Community Service and Career Fair involving over sixty non-profit and governmental organizations.

BUSINESS ADMINISTRATION EXPERIENCE

(handwritten note: Includes past work experience to show off transferable skills)

May Merchandising Co., New York, NY   1993-1994

Assistant Market Representative

Analyzed and recommended core assortments of sportswear for 320-unit department store chain. Predicted fashion trends, and made purchasing recommendations to management.

Mercantile Stores Co., Inc., Fairfield, OH   1990-1992

Associate Buyer

Coordinated purchases of sportswear from corporate office of 80-unit department store chain. Negotiate with vendors on price, delivery and allowances.

Department Manager

Motivated, trained and supervised sales associates.

EDUCATION

M.A., Counseling, May 1995 • Ohio State University, Columbus, OH

B.S. with Distinction, Marketing, 1990 • University Of Nebraska, Lincoln, NE

SKILLS

WordPerfect, Microsoft Word, DBase IV, Lotus 1-2-3

ANDREAS VIOSTA

15 Maple Place, #5
Hackensack, NJ 06600
(201) 999-8888

EDUCATION

B.S., Mechanical Engineering, 1994
University of the Phillipines, Manila

Relevant Courses

Machine Design
Created rubberband-powered cars capable of performing Figure 8's;
designed paper bridges able to support over ten pounds.

Project descriptions help bring courses to life

Turbo Pascal
Designed a program to determine the air-conditioning needs of
various interiors. Wrote a program to score bowling matches.

DESIGN EXPERIENCE

1993-1994
ACME Laboratories, Manila, Phillipines
Co-founder and Design Engineer

Designed a hammering machine for indenting steel bars, anelectric dryer for silk-
screen printedgarments, and a complete manufacturing line for quick acting
automotive battery terminal clamps. Fabricated all molds and tools. Trained and
supervised staff.

COMPUTER SKILLS

Computer skills are subdivided for a more effective presentation

Languages:	C, Turbo Pascal
Software:	DOS 5.0, Mac/OS, LOTUS 123, Quattro Pro, Excel, Pagemaker, Harvard Graphics 2.0, Flowcharting, Windows 3.1, WordPerfect 5.1
Hardware:	IBM PC/XT/AT 386, Macintosh

SALES EXPERIENCE

1994-Present
Sears, Roebuck and Co., Hackensack , NJ
Sales Associate

Top ranked salesperson in the Lawn & Garden and Sporting
Goods Departments. Received highest score possible on the Shop
and Check Service Evaluation Survey.

ACTIVITIES

Gears and Pinions, Association of Engineering Students

Permanent residency leaves no doubt that Andreas is permitted to work

Organized a university-wide contest to promote the preservation
of library resources. Solicited alumni to raise prize money.

Permanent Resident of the United States

LORRAINE J. TALISMAN

222 Seventh Avenue , Marietta, Ohio 45750   (614) 333-3333

Profile offers a concise introduction to capture the reader's attention

PROFILE

More than five years of experience providing for the needs of companion animals, farm livestock, and native and exotic wildlife in a variety of animal care facilities.

Skills-based format is a good choice

HIGHLIGHTS OF EXPERIENCE

Animal Care and Wildlife Rehabilitation

- Developed expertise in all areas of the care and treatment of injured, sick, and orphaned wildlife, including animal rescue, physical examinations, daily management of wounds and fractures, coordinating release of recovered wildlife, and hand-rearing baby mammals and birds.

- Completed International Wildlife Rehabilitation Council's Basic Skills Seminar.

- Expanded behavior training regimen for imprinted bald eagle at The Conservancy's Wildlife Center in Naples, Florida.

Environmental Education

- Conducted tours of The Conservancy's Wildlife Center for visitors of all ages. Provided information about wildlife rehabilitation and the wildlife of South Florida. Presented complex scientific concepts in an accessible, easy to grasp manner.

- Led interpretive and experiential outdoor education classes for children in the Summer Adventures program at Aullwood Audubon Center and Farm, Dayton, Ohio.

Training and Organizational Skills

- Trained and supervised numerous interns and volunteers. Taught basic medical skills, animal handling techniques, and facility maintenance. Contributed to the development of The Conservancy's volunteer training program.

- Assisted with organizing the International Wildlife Rehabilitation Council's 15th Annual Conference.

EDUCATION

Marietta College, Marietta, OH • Bachelor of Science, Biology, May 1993

Employers are listed first because Lorraine's titles don't have much clout

SELECTED WORK HISTORY

The Conservancy, Wildlife Rehabilitation Center, Naples, FL, Sr. Intern, 1994-Present

DuPont Washington Works Osprey Reintroduction Program, Blennerhasset Island, WV, Volunteer, 1994

The Cincinnati Zoo, Cincinnati, OH, Animal Care Department, Intern, 1993-1994

Chesapeake Wildlife Sanctuary, Bowie, MD, Wildlife Care Center, Intern, 1992

Aullwood Audubon Center & Farm, Dayton, OH, Environmental Educ. Intern, 1991

Animal Medical Center, New York, NY, Volunteer, 1990

Marietta Animal Hospital, Marietta, OH, Kennel Assistant, 1988-1989

CARLA DELACROIX
28 Ratchett Street
Denver, CO 11111
(888) 555-0000

PROFILE

- Ability to analyze disputes and conflicts impartially, and resolve them diplomatically; knowledgeable about arbitration, contracts, and labor law.

- Completing M.S. degree in Human Resource Management and Labor Relations.

- Elected as the youngest Chairperson of the Executive Board in the history of the Transport Workers Union, Local 553.

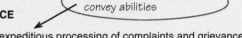

LABOR RELATIONS EXPERIENCE

- Solely responsible for the expeditious processing of complaints and grievances for 800 union members; served as official union spokesperson.

- Promoted the interests of flight attendants locally and nationally; safeguarded the individual and collective rights of all members; successfully lobbied Governor Cuomo to obtain unemployment benefits for flight attendants.

- Conducted legal research regarding labor disputes; interpreted contracts and prepared contract amendments; clarified rules and regulations for the union membership.

MANAGEMENT EXPERIENCE

- Organized and chaired numerous committees; oversaw publication of newsletter.

- Supervised up to six flight attendants; trained new personnel.

- Responsible for budget management and allocation.

EDUCATION

M.S., Human Resource Management and Labor Relations, May 1995
University of Denver, Denver, CO

- Center for Labor and Industrial Relations Scholarship

- Graduate Assistant to the Dean

Leadership Certification in Management and Labor Relations, 1990
Florida State University, Tallahassee, FL

B.A., English Literature and Marketing, 1986
McGill University, Montreal, Canada

WORK EXPERIENCE

Flight Attendant, United Airlines, 1986-present

Jan Nordstrom

West 24th Street Apt. A
San Francisco, CA 00011
Office (415) 999-9999
Home (415) 777-3333

Targeted heading relates directly to Jan's career goal

PUBLISHING EXPERIENCE

Elephant Books, San Francisco, CA
Customer Affairs and Sales Representative
1994-Present

Excellent use of quantification

- In charge of 68 distributor and retail book store accounts nationwide; assist with the development of new business.

- Sell and promote romance, true crime, action/adventure, and non-fiction titles. Forecast projected sales; prepare sales reports.

- Oversee the shipping of books to over 10,000 customers. Track merchandise, and forecast shipment and arrival dates. Efficiently and courteously resolve all disputes and discrepancies.

- Issue credit refunds and investigate returns for the Credit Department.

- Handle all aspects of catalog sales and promotions, accounting for over 800 orders monthly.

Company Booksellers, San Francisco, CA
Retail Sales Manager
1992-1994

Adverbs give reader a sense of how well Jan carried out his responsibilities

- Oversaw day-to-day retail operations; managed a staff of 10.

- Maintained and encouraged customer loyalty through the courteous and efficient resolution of disputes, complaints, and discrepancies; offered purchase recommendations to customers.

- Maintained inventory and transaction records via computer; regularly contacted publishers and distributors to ensure efficient processing of special orders.

- Boosted overall sales by improving various aspects of the overall retail environment; periodically surveyed competition to keep abreast of current retail trends.

- Administered daily cash and credit receipts.

EDUCATION

San Francisco State University, San Francisco, CA
Bachelor of Arts, English, May 1995
Major GPA: 3.75

LISA AVERY

9999 Jones Street • San Francisco, CA 99999 • 415-333-3333

PROFILE   Experienced project manager with strong background in architecture and design. Proven ability to initiate and maintain excellent relations with high end clientele. Skilled at developing new business contacts.

Profile conveys an image of a well-balanced professional

ARCHITECTURE/ DESIGN EXPERIENCE

1993-Present   **Charles M. Salter Associates, Inc.**, San Francisco, CA

Selected Projects Include:

Walt Disney Concert Hall, Frank Gehry & Associates
Disney /MGM Studios Europe, Marne-la Vallee

Liaison to architect; coordinated project research; reviewed drawings; assisted engineers with architectural projects; assisted with field measurements; translated technical terms from French to English.

Knoll International

Collaborated with designer and project manager in the conceptualization and development of the San Francisco showroom. Monitored construction; served as liaison to contractor; accessorized photo shoots.

Descriptions organized by project make Lisa's experience come alive

1992-1993   **The Richard Penney Group**, New York, NY

Selected Projects Include:

Atelier International Showroom, Washington, D.C.

Designer/Project Manager for showroom renovation. Coordinated with project architect and contractors; conducted client presentations; developed schematic design; altered existing textile display system; budgeting.

Sony Corporation, Regional Demonstration Exhibition Display

Designed finish and textile programs for exhibit system.

Details, Member Steelcase Design Partnership, WorkFlo

Collaborated on development of finish programs and product configurations; constructed study models for IBD Gold award-winning desk accessory line.

EDUCATION   Amherst College - BA, Fine Arts, 1992
Anna Baker Heap Prize for Urban Design Writing

SKILLS   Languages: Fluent in French

Computers: Excel, Microsoft Word, WordPerfect

Mary Baggio

111 East 20th Street, #0
New York, NY 10000
(212) 222-8888

Atlantic Motion Pictures, New York, NY

Coordinate shoots of commercials; ensure   that crew has access to all necessary supplies and equipment; check for color consistencyand image quality during supervised tapes transfers; maintain videotape library; liaison to vendors; appeared as talent in two NBC "Late Night"promos.

Broadcast Arts Productions, New York, NY

Coordinated live action shoots of commercials; organized animation cells to correspond with storyboards.

R. Greenberg, New York, NY

Served as on-stage talent coordinator in a series of consumer products commercials.

Videographer,

Freelance

Conceptualize, write, direct and shoot short videos.

additional experience

Assistant Copywriter, 1992

Mirabella Magazine, New York, NY

Created descriptions to accompany photographs of fashion accessories.

education

BFA, Painting, 1992

Miami University, Oxford, OH

skills

Rough cut editing of 3/4" video
Black & white photography
Experienced with a variety of video cameras
Microsoft Word for Macintosh

CARLA RIOJA
East Arrow St., #1
Durham, NC 10000
(222) 111-0000

DESIGN/FASHION EXPERIENCE

1993-Present   **Freelance Designer**, Durham. NC
- Design curtains, pillows and other home furnishings; use expertise to guide clients in the selection of fabric, style, color, and texture.
- Designed and constructed backpacks and evening bags.
- Implemented bi-coastal marketing and promotional campaigns; coordinated promotional/sales events.
- Major clients include Fred Seigal, Santa Monica, CA, and Wrights, Manhattan Beach, CA.

(handwritten note: Mentions clients to establish credibility)

Summer 1993   **Keeble Cavaco & Duka**, Raleigh, NC
Freelance Coordinator
- Organized invitations and RSVP follow-up for fashion shows for various designers including Richard Tyler and Anna Sui.
- Coordinated seating arrangements for media and retailers.
- Planned and facilitated a variety of special events including receptions, openings, and book signings.

(handwritten note: Name dropping can be useful in fields like fashion design)

1992   **The Surrogate Chef**, Durham, NC
Events Coordinator
- Catered events for up to 3,000 people; clients included major corporations as well as celebrities.
- In charge of event styling; planned and selected color schemes, flower arrangements, tablecloths, place settings, and props.

ADDITONAL EXPERIENCE

1988-1991   **American Airlines**, New York, NY
International Flight Attendant
- Responsible for the comfort and safety of up to 350 passengers per flight.
- Provide efficient and courteous service to a diverse clientele.

EDUCATION

Duke University, Durham, NC
Bachelor of Arts, Visual Arts, May 1995
Honors: Art Scholarship granted by the Neptunian Women's Club

Study Abroad   **L'Ecole du Louvre**, **Le Sorbonne**, Paris, France
Studies included interior design, art history, and French

AFS International Exchange Program, Minas Gerais, Brazil

(handwritten note: Study abroad demonstrates Carla's awareness of other cultures)

LANGUAGES

Conversational French

ROY ROMARIO

1 Irving Street
Evanston, IL 10000
(222) 555-7777

EDUCATION

Northwestern University, Evanston, IL
Bachelor of Science, *Management & Finance*, May 1996

Overall GPA: 3.24
- Will complete degree in three years.

Sends a message that Roy has drive

Relevant Courses

Management	Computer Based Systems
Operations Research	Accounting
Organizational Behavior	Statistics

Activities

Activities demonstrate leadership skills

Science Fiction Club, *Vice President-elect*
- Reviewed and selected material published in the annual magazine.

Society for Creative Anachronism, *Treasurer*
- Oversaw the club's budget; participated in the development of the club's award-winning programming activities.

Connections, Alumni Mentor Program, *Mentee*
- Meet regularly with alumni to discuss academic, career, and business issues.

Tutor, Operations Research, Statistics, Computer Based Systems

Netzah, *Activities Counselor*

EXPERIENCE

Industria de Fitas Elasticas Estrela, Sao Paulo, Brazil
Production Supervisor, Summer 1994

- Analyzed the production process, and devised strategies to increase production efficiency for this manufacturer of elastic bands and Velcro.
- Performed general administrative tasks.

COMPUTER SKILLS

IBM: DBase III, Quattro Pro, Lotus, Microsoft Windows

Macintosh: Excel, WordPerfect, Microsoft Word

LANGUAGES

- Fluent in English, French, and Portuguese
- Strong knowledge of Italian
- Understanding of written and spoken Spanish

Language skills should be a bonus for international companies

TARA ANNE DIONNE
(213) 999-0000

Height	5'3"	*Eyes*	Brown
Weight	106	*Voice*	Soprano
Hair	Brown	*Age Range*	20-35

Vital statistics are crucial for acting and modeling

THEATRE

THE MYSTERY OF EDWIN DROOD	Rosa Bud	Duncan Theatre
HAIR	Chrissy	Utah Rep
RAGS	Rebecca	Duncan Theatre
PIRATES OF PENZANCE	Mabel	Duncan Theatre
SHE LOVES ME	Amalia	Village Players
LOOSE ENDS	Susan	Duncan Theatre
ELIZABETH & ESSEX	Lady Anne	Utah Rep
FIORELLO!	Nina/Florence	Utah Rep
RED NOSES	Camille	Duncan Theatre
YOU CAN'T TAKE IT WITH YOU	Alice	Village Players
NO SEX PLEASE, WE'RE BRITISH	Barbara	Village Players

Selected credits help establish Tara's range as an actor

TRAINING

ACTING	**Bachelor of Arts**, *Drama*, Utah State University, May 1995 Gately-Poole Acting Studio Ginger Friedman Audition Workshop, Gillian Moore Commercial Workshop FPTA Advanced Acting Workshop
VOICE	Winston Clark Patricia Adams-Johnson
DANCE	Scott Shettleroe Utah Ballet (ballet, jazz) Salt Lake Ballet Center (ballet, jazz, tap)
MUSICAL THEATRE	Musical Theatre Works Conservatory Donald Oliver

Names of coaches can sometimes help open doors

SPECIAL TALENTS

Dialects (English, Brooklyn, Southern, French), Hair & Make up, Costuming

LARRY FITZPATRICK

Graphic presentation suitable for a creative field like photography

West 12th Street, #10, Washington, D.C. 10000, 222.222.2222

PHOTOGRAPHY EXPERIENCE

Innovative format permits Larry to stress skills in addition to listing employer information

Job titles omitted because most of Larry's work is freelance

Associated Press   *1994-Present*
Printed black and white photos to accompany news releases in publications such as *The New York Times*, *the Washington Post*, and the *Herald Tribune*. Handled trafficking and proofreading of all AP third-party graphics over various networks.

Smithsonian Institute   *1993*
Produced black and white prints for journalists and delegations.

Laumont Color Lab   *1992-1993*
Reproduced color correct slides from originals; mounted and packaged slides for promotional purposes; clients included PBS and HBO.

FILM / VIDEO EXPERIENCE

MTV Networks   *1994-Present*
Production Assistant for rockumentaries on Aerosmith, Janet Jackson, and Whitney Houston; viewed and logged tapes.

Collective for Living Cinema   *1993-1994*
Teacher's Assistant for beginning filmmaking workshops; taught students use of Super 8mm equipment; facilitated discussion groups. Coordinated screenings, projected films, oversaw box office.

GALLERY EXPERIENCE

Aperture Foundation Gallery   *Summer 1992*
Matted, framed, and hung works for exhibits by artists such as Mapplethorpe, Eggleston, and Strand. Coordinated gallery openings; liaison between clients and artists.

EDUCATION

Georgetown University
Bachelor of Fine Arts, Photography, 1993

American University
Coursework in Video Production, 1994

ROSE BERGER
14 West 2nd Street, Apt. F
New York, NY 10000
(212) 444-0000

EDUCATION

Phillips Beth Israel School of Nursing, New York, NY
Associate in Applied Science Degree, June 1995
Dean's List: 1993-1995
Hillman Scholarship: 1993-1995

State University of New York at Cortland, Cortland, NY
Bachelor of Arts, Secondary French Education

HEALTH CARE EXPERIENCE

Summer '94-Present   **Beth Israel Medical Center**, New York, NY
Student Nurse Extern, P.A.C.U.

Perform the following under the supervision of a Registered Nurse: Admit patients to ambulatory and in-patient units; monitor vital signs; remove IVs and catheters; administer glucose tests, urinetests, and enemas; perform suctioning; teach crutch walking; conduct discharge teaching; attend in-service training sessions.

1992-1993   **Lenox Hill Hospital**, New York, NY
Volunteer, AIDS Unit

Provided companionship to patients, their families, and significant others. Assisted patients with feeding and personal hygiene.

1986-1987   **Children's Hospital Medical Center**, Washington D.C.
Volunteer, Adolescent Unit

Played with and comforted children, most of whom were suffering from leukemia, cystic fibrosis, or anorexia nervosa. Coordinated and led group excursions. Provided general assistance to nurses.

RECENT PROFESSIONAL EXPERIENCE

1989-1992   **Simon's Hardware**, New York, NY
Bath Showroom Manager

Trained and supervised staff. Diplomatically resolved customer complaints. Purchased and maintained inventory.

1987-1988   **Coopers & Lybrand**, New York, NY
Office Services Coordinator

Provided administrative and office services support to 200 tax partners and professionals.

PROFESSIONAL AFFILIATIONS

1992-Present   National Student Nurses Association

CHRIS JONES

111 Stonebury Avenue
Providence, RI 00000
(444) 222-1111

OBJECTIVE

Position in Commercial Banking.

EDUCATION

Fordham University, Bronx, NY
Bachelor of Arts, Economics, June 1995

• Financed 40% of college expenses through part-time employment.

List of courses supports Chris's objective

Relevant Courses: Money and Banking
Micro- and Macroeconomics Information
SystemsStatistics

ACTIVITIES

Point Guard, Junior Varsity Basketball Team, 1991-1994
Member, Economics Club
Tutor, Upward Bound Program
Member, Kappa Delta Rho fraternity

Varied activities show Chris to be extemely well rounded

EXPERIENCE

Bookkeeper, Summer 1994
Little Tree Nurseries, Seekonk, MA

Effective use of power verbs to convey accomplishments

• Designed spreadsheets utilizing Excel to maintain accounts and sales receivable.

• Accurately entered data from incoming checks.

Intern, Business Development, Summer 1993
Rhode Island Dept. of Economic Development, Providence, RI

• Researched and prepared a written report on all aspects of the Rhode Island fishing industry to assist government officials with evaluating statewide policy.

• Reviewed and evaluated applications for businesses seeking a minority status designation.

• Compiled information on federal funding guidelines for the Rhode Island Institute of Mental Health.

• Maintained a database of potential business sites.

Telemarketer, Summer 1992
American Safe Water Systems, Lincoln, RI

• Convinced consumers via cold calling to schedule appointments for demonstrations of a water purification system.

COMPUTER SKILLS

Lotus 1-2-3, Excel, DBase, WordPerfect, Microsoft Word

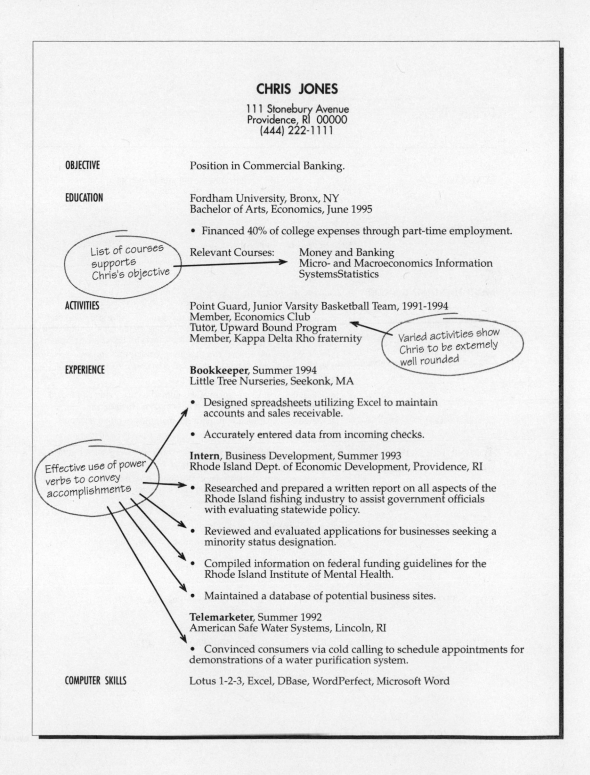

PERRY WEISS　　401 East Street
Atlanta, GA 00021
(222) 999-9999

SUMMARY

Profile establishes credibility

Over three years of experience in the apparel industry with proven ability in merchandising, sales, and office management. Extremely organized, efficient, and resourceful.

EXPERIENCE

Associate Merchandiser, 1992-Present
Elite Sportswear, Ltd., Atlanta, GA

Elite is a $30 million women's sportswear manufacturer.

Since company is relatively unknown, the summary here is helpful

MERCHANDISING/SALES

Skills-based subheadings guide the reader to Perry's strength's

- Consistently locate the most cost-effective materials by making frequent excursions to fabric companies, fabric expos, and trim shows.
- Research fashion and market trends through extensive shopping of department and specialty stores in the U.S. and Europe, and careful review of fashion magazines, trade publications, and catalogs.
- Present recommendations regarding fabric, color, print, and style selection at weekly merchandising meetings.
- Design presentation and concept boards.
- Initiated, developed, and maintained numerous accounts; conducted extensive phone follow-up to ensure buyer satisfaction.
- Designed and distributed promotional materials to target accounts.

ADMINISTRATION

- Accurately maintained all company records including sales figures, purchase orders, and production tickets.
- Coordinated with production and shipping managers to ensure that all accounts received the correct shipments in a timely fashion; diplomatically resolved order discrepancies.
- Devised and implemented a filing system which resulted in improved office efficiency and productivity.
- Interviewed prospective administrative personnel and made hiring recommendations.
- Trained and supervised a staff of three.

EDUCATION

Bachelor of Arts, Cum Laude, Psychology, May 1994
Emory University, Atlanta, GA

SKILLS

WordPerfect 5.1, Typing, reading knowledge of Italian

SHEILA L'AMOUR

35 West End Avenue   (212) 777-7777 - Residence
New York, NY 10000   (212) 999-9999 - Business

SUMMARY

(handwritten note: Summary introduces Sheila as a real dynamo)

* Proven ability in Strategic Planning, Process Analysis, Needs Analysis and Proposal Development.
* Results-oriented team player with excellent analytical, problem solving, and organizational skills.
* Familiar and comfortable working with cutting edge computer technology.
* Currently pursuing an MBA at New York University while working full-time.

CONSULTING EXPERIENCE

(handwritten note: Targeted heading allows Sheila to list her most relevant experience first)

Coopers & Lybrand, Management Consulting Services, New York, NY 1991-1994
Associate, Information Technology Practice

* As member of project team, recommended and implemented technological business solutions for such clients as AT&T, Prodigy, Citibank, and WNET.

* Member of the Coopers & Lybrand management transition team. Diplomatically communicated employment-related concerns between staff and upper management.

* Developed and implemented a mentor program for new hires.

(handwritten note: Quantification makes accomplishments stand out)

ADDITIONAL WORK EXPERIENCE

New York University, Office of Career Services, New York, NY 1994-Present
Recruitment Coordinator

* Manage all aspects of the on-campus recruitment program including coordination and scheduling of over 6,000 student interviews and 50 company presentations annually. Establish, develop, and maintain close working relationships with executives from over 200 organizations.

* Assisted with the design, development, and implementation of an innovative relational recruitment database.

EDUCATION

New York University, Graduate School of Business Administration, New York, NY
Master of Business Administration, Marketing, May 1997

Rutgers University, New Brunswick, NJ
Bachelor of Arts, Psychology with an emphasis in Organizational Behavior, May 1990

TECHNICAL SKILLS

Hardware: IBM PC and Compatibles, Macintosh

Software: Lotus 1-2-3, Excel, 4th Dimension, DBase IV,
                 Relational Report Writer, FileMaker, WordPerfect, Microsoft Word

Profile establishes Mojo as a seasoned pro

MOJO MELKWEG

East Barnacle Street • Las Vegas, NV 10000 • 222.888.8888

PROFILE

Professional experience in Marketing, Operations, and Applied Computer Technology plus a solid academic background in Information Systems and International Business. Ability to conceptualize the big picture, as well as pay careful attention to every last detail. Excel at organizing, coordinating, and managing projects.

EXPERIENCE

Avon Products, Inc.   *Marketing Intern*

Provide administrative and technical support to the Planning, Analysis, and Research team. Assist with the coordination and moderation of focus groups conducted nationwide; handle logistics, collect qualitative data to be used in forecasting. Contributed to the development of a database designed to store information collected during quantitative and qualitative clinics. Maintain database, clean data, and classify information to be entered. **1993-Present**

Digital Equipment Corporation   *Project Specialist*

Oversaw course enrollment for a 10-room training facility serving up to 100 students per week. On-line supervisor for 15 Boston-based registrars. Identified and resolved issues concerning payment, revenue reconciliation, and invoicing. Troubleshooting required extensive contact with key personnel in Administration, Sales, Education, and Finance. Recipient of the *Digital Equipment Corporation Excellence Award for Service.* Promoted twice. **1990-1993**

Free-Room UK, England   *Account Executive - Key Accounts*

Sold over 500K in consumer incentives and sales promotional items to Marketing Directors of companies throughout the United Kingdom. Arranged board meetings and presentations in conjunction with Sales Director. Served as key contact for resales and troubleshooting for major clients. Expanded target markets; supervised Research Assistants. Promoted twice. **1986-1988**

EDUCATION

University of Nevada, Las Vegas
Bachelor of Science, Information Systems/International Business, Summer 1995

Worked an average of 30 hours weekly while attending classes full-time.
Overall GPA: 3.5

Demonstrates an impressive work ethic

Honors: School of Business Scholarship

              Class Representative, School of Continuing Education Class of '93. Awarded to the student with the highest GPA in the graduating class.

SKILLS

C Programming, Access, Excel, Lotus Organizer, Microsoft Word, E-Mail

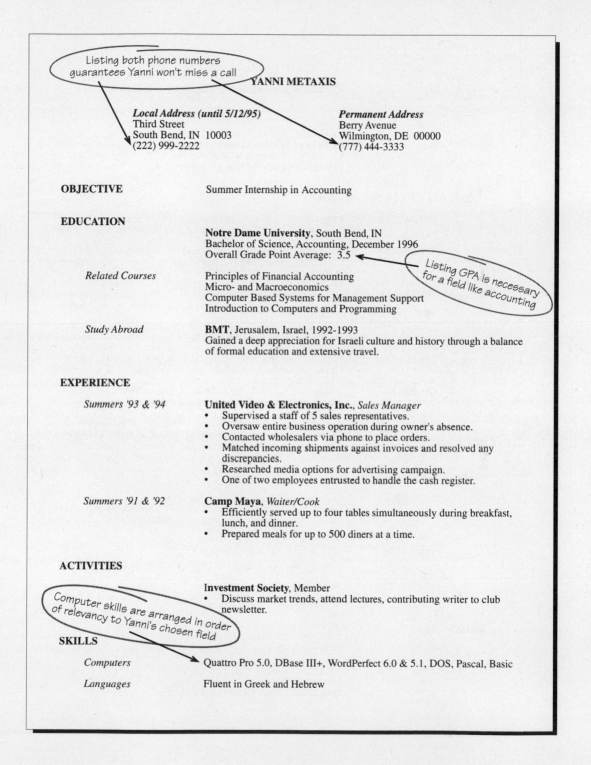

Listing both phone numbers guarantees Yanni won't miss a call

YANNI METAXIS

Local Address (until 5/12/95)
Third Street
South Bend, IN 10003
(222) 999-2222

Permanent Address
Berry Avenue
Wilmington, DE 00000
(777) 444-3333

OBJECTIVE   Summer Internship in Accounting

EDUCATION

Notre Dame University, South Bend, IN
Bachelor of Science, Accounting, December 1996
Overall Grade Point Average: 3.5 ◄

Listing GPA is necessary for a field like accounting

Related Courses   Principles of Financial Accounting
Micro- and Macroeconomics
Computer Based Systems for Management Support
Introduction to Computers and Programming

Study Abroad   **BMT**, Jerusalem, Israel, 1992-1993
Gained a deep appreciation for Israeli culture and history through a balance
of formal education and extensive travel.

EXPERIENCE

Summers '93 & '94   **United Video & Electronics, Inc.**, *Sales Manager*
- Supervised a staff of 5 sales representatives.
- Oversaw entire business operation during owner's absence.
- Contacted wholesalers via phone to place orders.
- Matched incoming shipments against invoices and resolved any
  discrepancies.
- Researched media options for advertising campaign.
- One of two employees entrusted to handle the cash register.

Summers '91 & '92   **Camp Maya**, *Waiter/Cook*
- Efficiently served up to four tables simultaneously during breakfast,
  lunch, and dinner.
- Prepared meals for up to 500 diners at a time.

ACTIVITIES

Investment Society, Member
- Discuss market trends, attend lectures, contributing writer to club
  newsletter.

Computer skills are arranged in order of relevancy to Yanni's chosen field

SKILLS

Computers   Quattro Pro 5.0, DBase III+, WordPerfect 6.0 & 5.1, DOS, Pascal, Basic

Languages   Fluent in Greek and Hebrew

RITA WILSON

100 Bridge Street • Seattle, WA 00000 • (999) 333-0000

EDUCATION

Bachelor of Science, Health and Physical Education, December 1995
University of Washington, Seattle, WA
Dean's List: four semesters

Thumbnail descriptions allows inclusion of several positions

FITNESS TRAINING / SPORTS MANAGEMENT EXPERIENCE

Targeted headings stress Rita's greatest strengths

1994-Present	Chiropractor's Assistant, The Winning Team, Cedar Knoll, WA Assist with treating patients; provide laser and ultrasound treatments.
1994-Present	Recreation Center Manager, University of Washington Supervise operation of 5,000 square foot facility used by 200 athletes daily.
1992-Present	Trainer, University of Washington Design and implement rehabilitation programs for injured athletes.
Summer 1994	Instructor/Counselor, Mighty Burners Speed Camp, Tacoma, WA Coached aspiring sprinters, ages 10-13.
Summer 1993	Program Assistant, Job Training Partnership Act, Seattle, WA Developed and coordinated physcial fitness programs for youngsters.
Summer 1992	Trainer, Ted Rocks Health and Fitness, Seattle, WA Trained young adults in proper weight training techniques.
1991	Cross Country and Track Manager, University of Washington Coordinated meets; answered recruits' inquiries; performed various administrative tasks.

COUNSELING / TEACHING EXPERIENCE

1992-1994	University of Washington Educational Opportunity Program Provided academic counseling to EOP students. Developed CHOICES program to facilitate the acquisition of problem solving skills for inner city youth and adults.
1993-1994	Student Athletes for Education (SAFE) Visited local high schools to promote the benefits of a college education.
1992-1993	Seattle School District Intern Health and Physical Education Instructor, grades 1-10.

ATHLETIC HONORS

1995	West Regional Track & Field Champion, Long Jump and 100 Meter HH
1994	NCAA's Washington Athlete of the Year
1994	World Indoor Track Championship Qualifier

DANA WILLIAMS

22 Sparrow Lane   Hartsdale, New York 10000   914-666-6666

SOCIAL SERVICE EXPERIENCE

Substance Abuse Counselor / HIV Program Coordinator, 1993-Present
Lafayette Medical Management, New York, NY

(handwritten note: Numbers help convey the magnitude of Dana's workload)

- Manage a caseload of 70 clients currently on methadone maintenance. Provide individual and group counseling. Focus on issues such as goal setting, employment, education, nutrition, health care, and hygiene.

- Created the HIV Counseling Program which services over 200 participants. Coordinate weekly rap sessions, arrange guest lectures and staff training, organize various group activities, distribute condoms and safe sex literature, and conduct pre- and post-HIV test counseling. Supervise two assistants.

- Prepare monthly, quarterly, semi-annual, and annual reports based on case reviews. Monitor the results of weekly toxicological/urine profiles and take action as necessary. Conduct intake interviews with newly accepted program participants.

Group Home Counselor, 1992
Abbot House, Irvington, NY

- Counseled 10 emotionally disturbed boys, ages 12 to 17.

(handwritten note: Bullets organized by general themes make life easy on the reader)

- Oversaw the boys' educational development. Met regularly with classroom teachers, monitored the boys' academic progress, provided and arranged for tutoring, and organized educational field trips and various cultural excursions.

Co-Founder, 1992-Present
Liberian Association for Unity and Development (LAUD), New York, NY

- Founding member of this non-profit organization dedicated to promoting awareness of Liberian culture and providing humanitarian aid in the U.S. and abroad.

- Designed and implemented a mentor program offering 12-18 year-olds the opportunity to meet weekly with carefully selected role models to learn about Liberian culture and values.

EDUCATION

Bachelor of Arts, **Psychology**, December 1993
Long Island University, Brookville, NY

- Financed part of college education through steady part-time employment.

PROFESSIONAL DEVELOPMENT

- Overview Course in HIV/AIDS Infection

- Pre- and Post-Test Training Course in HIV Counseling

(handwritten note: Professional Development category demonstrates Dana's commitment to her field)

- Big Brother/Big Sister Mentorship Development Training Seminar

lianna maria white

15 River Street, Apt. #3 Pittsburgh, PA 10000 (222) 555-5555

education

(handwritten note, circled: Stresses education to compensate for lack of career related experience)

Carnegie Mellon University, Pittsburgh, PA
Bachelor of Arts, Politics/History, May 1996

Minor: Spanish
Major GPA: 3.2
Honors: College of Arts and Science Scholarship

• Financed 50% of college costs through various part time jobs.

Relevant Courses

Power and Politics in America	American Constitutional Law
International Politics	Women in Law
Comparative Politics	United States History

(handwritten note, circled: List of courses gives reader a sense of her political interests and knowledge base)

experience

1994 - Present

Carnegie Mellon University, Pittsburgh, PA
Admissions Ambassador

Conduct campus tours for up to 25 prospective students and their parents. Respond to phone inquiries regarding admissions and specific academic programs. Represent Carnegie Mellon at open houses and other special events. Provide administrative support within the Admissions Office.

Fall 1993

Investors Associates, Pittsburgh, PA
Sales Assistant

Supported sales efforts of brokers by maintaining up to date client records and daily logs of stock purchases and sales. Coordinated follow-up mailings to clients.

Summer 1993

Edward Isaacs & Company (CPAs), Pittsburgh, PA
Telemarketer

Laid the groundwork for the sale of financial software by convincing potential clients to register for a free evaluation of their computer systems. Heavy phone contact with high level executives. Maintained client leads via computer.

activities

Democratic Club - Organized and promoted club activities and events; assisted with voter registration drive.

Pre-Law Society, Member

ESL Tutor

skills

Languages: Fluent in Spanish
Computers: Macintosh: Microsoft Works, IBM: WordPerfect 5.1

interests

(handwritten note, circled: List of interests establishes Lianna as well-rounded and worldly)

International travel (have visited several countries in Central America and Europe), flute, art museums, ethnic fairs and festivals, Spanish literature, foreign films, African history

LOLITA TRUJILLO

24 Fourth Street
Austin, TX 07777
(222) 888-6666

Profile offers a broad overview of Lolita's experience and abilities

PROFILE

Experienced researcher and educator with strong academic background in the History of Art and Latin America. Excel at public relations, customer service and sales. Skilled at photography, layout, painting, and drawing. Bilingual in English and Spanish.

EDUCATION

M.A., Latin American and Carribean Studies, May 1995
University of Texas, Austin, TX
Co-coordinate a campus speaker series featuring Latin American artists.

B.A., Fine Arts, with a concentration in Painting, May 1993
Jersey City State College, Jersey City, NJ

MUSEUM EXPERIENCE

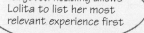

Targeted heading allows Lolita to list her most relevant experience first

Children's Museum of New York, New York, NY
Exhibit Research Intern
Spring 1991
Conducted research on Armenian culture and history for the exhibit: "Look and Look Again: Children's Artwork from Armenia." Liaison to the Armenian community; obtained and catalogued authentic Armenian artifacts and ensured their safe return.

ADDITIONAL EXPERIENCE

Carolee, Austin, TX
Sales Specialist
1993-Present

Description communicates a wide variety of skills for a seemingly mundane position

Assist a varied clientele with selecting costume and fashion jewelry; Collaborate with cosmetic consultants to enhance the customer's overall image; design sales displays.

El Especial, Union City, NJ
Advertising Design Assistant
1989
Developed various paste-ups, layouts, and designs.

ACTIVITIES

Peer Tutor, Jersey City State College
Tutored four college students in English grammar and writing.

Eliane Jobim

15 East 6th Street, #2
Miami, FL 10000
(212) 333-6666

Profile

√ Four years of experience in the fashion industry. Significant exposure to retail and wholesale.
√ Expertise in public relations, special events, marketing, and product development.
√ Keen awareness of new trends and styles. Proven ability to meet deadlines.

Public Relations/ Special Events Experience

Gucci, Assistant to Director of Publicity & Special Events: 1993-Present

√ Wrote press releases for newspapers, magazines, and television.
√ Heavy contact with media representatives; served as information broker.
√ Organized fashion shows and store events. Assembled outfits for fashion shoots.

Marketing/ Product Development Experience

Liz Claiborne, Assistant to Vice President of Design: 1991-1993

√ Shopped numerous retail establishments to determine current fashion trends.
√ Researched and wrote monthly fashion forecasting reports. Utilized spreadsheet software to aid with line planning.
√ Assisted with conceptualizing and preparing presentation boards and advertising collateral including, "mood tags," store mailers, and corporate mailers for specialty shops. Developed promotional giveaways for buyers.
√ Researched colors for new lines and collaborated on the setting of color standards.

Skills

Lotus 1-2-3, Paradox, WordPerfect 5.1, Magic, Platinum. Fluent in Greek.

Education

The Berkeley College, B.S., Fashion Marketing & Management: 1993

CHAPTER 9

TAKING YOUR RESUME ON THE ROAD

You've created your very first trashproof resume. Congratulations. Give yourself a big pat on the back. We'll bet you're just raring to go and print hundreds of copies of that little sucker so you can begin your job hunt in earnest. Well, slow down just a minute. There's still some unfinished business to attend to. Before you go waste your money on fancy paper, make sure that your resume is completely—and we mean completely—error-free. One little mistake and all your hard work could be for nought. Enlist a couple of good proofreaders to give your resume the twice over. Only after it has received their seal of approval should you prepare to have it printed.

THE PAPER CHASE

Once you get the green light, you'll need to pick out paper and envelopes. This could easily be an all-day affair, as paper and envelopes come in a mind-boggling array of colors, shades, textures, and weights. The best thing to do when shopping for paper stock is to bring along a friend who has both a good eye and some common sense.

Unless you're applying for a position in which your aesthetic judgment is being carefully evaluated, it doesn't make a great deal of difference what kind of paper you choose for your resume. Odds are that you're not going to be hired for your taste in paper.

You can't go wrong with a box of standard twenty-four pound, hundred-percent cotton fiber paper. Just make sure it's 8 1/2 x 11 inches in size, and that it's laser friendly. Textured papers are fine as well, as long as the texture isn't so pronounced that it overpowers your text. Patterned papers, on the other hand, such as parchment, tend to be quite distracting to the reader and are not recommended.

In terms of color, stay on the neutral side. White, off-white, ivory, light beige, and pale gray are all perfectly acceptable. The advantage of white is that it reproduces well when faxed or photocopied, whereas colored paper tends to come out muddled-looking. Pure white, though, is highly reflective and tends to be quite harsh on the reader's eyes.

PRINTING

For the best resolution and quality, laser printing is the only way to go. If it's too costly for you to have all of your resumes laser printed, you could instead make photocopies, as you need them, from a laser-printed original. If you choose this path, just be sure to tell the folks at the copy shop that your life depends on the quality of the print job, and that you would appreciate it if they give the glass on the machine a good cleaning before printing your resumes. Also have them show you the first copy in the run before they print the rest of the job. This will allow you to make sure that your resume is properly aligned and free of spots, streaks, and any other imperfections.

Never print more resumes than you are ready to send out at one time. Printing ten to fifteen copies is a reasonable start (unless you are attending a large career fair or submitting resumes to your career planning office, in which case you must print as many as necessary). If you had any notion of doing a mass mailing, drop it. Mass mailings have been proven to be highly ineffective. Dump a hundred or so identical resumes and cover letters into the mail box and you might as well throw them in the trash. You will obtain much better results by individually tailoring your resumes to the needs of each prospective employer. Finally, printing your resume in small batches allows you to incorporate the suggestions of employers, counselors, and contacts for future versions.

ENVELOPES

To make your package look really professional, use envelopes that match your resume paper. The jury is still out on whether it makes a difference if you use standard business envelopes or the larger 9 x 12 inch envelopes. The advantage of the latter size is that when the recruiter opens your package, your resume and letter will be nice and flat. This benefit may be outweighed, however, by the fact that the larger envelopes are more costly and may require additional postage.

Whichever type of envelope you use, it is important that you print the recipient's address legibly and correctly, or your resume may never reach its destination. The address can be typed, laser printed, or hand written (provided you have good penmanship). Sometimes handwriting provides a welcome personal touch and ensures that the contents do not fall into the junk mail category. Use whichever printing method is most convenient for you. Also, don't forget to include your return address on the envelope.

THE COVER LETTER

You're two-thirds of the way home. Your resume is printed, your envelopes are all set, and now the only thing you're missing is a cover letter. What's a cover letter, you ask? The cover letter serves as a personalized introduction to your resume. It briefly explains who you are, why you're writing the employer, and what you have to offer. The letter is comprised of three main sections: the opening, the sales pitch, and the closing.

The cover letter is a strange animal. Depending on which employer you speak with, it is either pivotal or irrelevant. Some employers won't even bother reading your resume if your cover letter doesn't arouse their curiosity. Others won't bother reading your cover letter until after they've glanced at your resume, and even then they will only give it a quick read. That said, we believe cover letters are still vital to the success of your job search, and should accompany every resume you send out.

> **No Dogs Allowed**
>
> *"Some of the cover letters I receive are so silly. I recall one that had a picture of the applicant's dog on it. The letter, supposedly written by the dog, said, 'please give my owner a job because she's driving me crazy at home.' Now some employers might think that's cute, but others are going to throw it right in the trash. It's a gamble that's not worth taking. The best cover letters state specifically what you want to do, respond point by point to the ad that has been placed, and show that you're a team player."*
>
> —Jim Berman, Director of Research
> WBBM-TV, Chicago

Get a Name

Your letter should be no more than a page in length, written in standard business format. It should always be addressed to a specific individual within the organization, unless you're responding to a blind ad which only lists a box number. If you're writing unsolicited (in other words, you don't know if a position is available) and don't have a contact name, call the organization to find out to whom your letter and resume should be sent. Or, if you pulled a contact name out of a directory or magazine, always call the organization to verify that this person is still employed. While on the phone make sure to ask for your contact's official title (it may have changed), as well as the correct spelling of his name.

Beware the Gatekeepers

When writing to an organization unsolicited, it is generally best to send your letter and resume both to the head of the department that most interests you, and to the human resources or personnel department. This is particularly true in large bureaucratic organizations. Individual department heads often have a better sense of their hiring needs than the people in human resources, who are saddled with the unenviable task of dealing with the staffing concerns of the entire organization. The department head will probably scrutinize your resume more closely, especially if she anticipates having an opening in the near future. This is not to say that you should avoid contacting human resources altogether, but simply that you should be aware that unless they are trying to fill a specific opening, your letter and resume may get lost in the shuffle.

Consider this example. Several years ago, there were six counselors in the career planning office of a large, bureaucratic university. One day, the director received an unsolicited letter of inquiry from a very strong candidate. Although there were no openings at that time, the director kept the letter on file in the event that a position became available. As luck would have it for the applicant, a few months later a job did open up. The candidate was invited for an interview, and eventually was offered the position. Had the applicant originally sent her letter of inquiry to the human resources department instead of to the director of career planning, the story might not have had such a happy ending. Odds are that human resources would have filed the applicant's letter away for "future reference," since no opening existed at the time they received it. There would have been only a slight chance they would have forwarded the letter to the director of career planning once the position opened up.

GRAND OPENING

Now that you've figured out who you're writing to, you need to come up with an opening. The opening should include why you're writing, where you heard about the position, and who you are. If you met with the employer previously or were referred by someone he knows well, make sure to point this out. Dropping an important name could be your express ticket in the door, so this is no time to feel guilty about knowing people in high places.

Opening—Referral

I am writing at the suggestion of your colleague, Frank Jones, who informed me that you are in need of a Marketing Research Assistant. As I have just completed my B.S. in Marketing at Arizona State, and plan to launch a career in market research, the position at your firm sounds ideal. Please consider me as an applicant.

Opening—Previously Met With Employer

It was a pleasure speaking with you on Tuesday at the Michigan State Career Fair. As you may recall, I have recently completed my B.S. in Management and have over three years of retail experience. I believe I can make a strong contribution to Lord and Taylor, and would like to be considered for a spot in your management training program.

Opening—Response to an Ad

I am writing to express my interest in the position of Banana Peeler which you advertised in last Sunday's issue of the Orangutan Times. I will be completing my degree in Banana Peeling this semester at the Honolulu Institute and will be available for work by May 15th.

Unsolicited Inquiry

Since I arrived here from outer space my life's ambition has been to write for *The National Enquirer*. I have read your paper every week for the past ten years. Despite having been raised on Mars, I mastered the English language in only two days, and recently completed my B.A. in Journalism at the University of Missouri. If you can use a talented, young, energetic Martian journalist on your staff, I am ready to give everything I've got to guarantee the continued success of the *Enquirer*.

Some ads ask for salary requirements and/or salary history in addition to a cover letter. The conventional wisdom has been to avoid providing this information at such a premature stage. The rationale was that nothing good could come of complying with a request designed to screen out applicants who are either too expensive or too cheap. It was recommended that you express confidence that you would receive a wage that is both commensurate with your qualifications and the demands of the position. It was assumed that if the employer was enticed by your credentials, he would contact you even if you didn't list salary requirements.

James Loree, an Assistant Vice President at Moody's Investor Services, looks at this issue from the employer's perspective. "Now that I'm on the other side of the fence, I've changed my mind about this. Listing salary requirements can be helpful to both the job hunter and the employer because it helps to establish whether there is a good match. Listing salary history is especially beneficial for the job hunter who has demonstrated consistent salary growth over the years. It shows the employer that this person is on a fast track. The important thing is to do your homework on your target industry, and make sure that the range you list is within reason for the position you've applied for."

THE SALES PITCH

The body of your letter must show the employer through concrete examples why you're qualified for the position in which you're interested. Vague references to generic skills won't cut it. You need to demonstrate point by point that you have the qualifications required. Try not to reiterate what's on your resume. Instead, focus on just a few specific accomplishments that are most relevant to the employer's needs. Emphasize, for example, the fact that you already have practical experience in the field, or that you recently earned a degree in a closely related subject area. Also, try to make it clear that you know something about the organization and why you'd like to work for them. Let your enthusiasm and team orientation shine through. Remember, you're trying to make a positive impression. To paraphrase John F. Kennedy, "ask not what the company can do for you, ask what you can do for the company."

There's no need to be cute, humorous, or overly creative, unless the position you're seeking requires these qualities. If that's the case, then you might want to try a more innovative approach to your cover letter. Try writing it as you would a press release, direct mail piece, playbill, baseball card, or "wanted" poster. Use your imagination.

It is easier to write a strong sales pitch when responding to an advertised opening, since the ad usually clearly states the key requirements for the job. However, if you're writing to an organization that doesn't necessarily have a current opening, you'll need to do some serious research first. Try to gather as much information as possible about the organization to gain a sense of what their needs are and where you might fit. Attempt to set up as many informational interviews as possible with professionals in your target field, and ask them what would be the most effective way to approach your prospective employer. Be patient and don't write your letter until you have a clear idea of how you want to position yourself.

Now It's Time to Say Goodbye

In closing your cover letter, your goal is to ask for an interview, and politely thank the employer for taking the time to consider you for employment. There is no need to drag this out. Just get right to the point. You could even state that you will be following up with a phone call in a specified period of time. Also, if you are writing to an employer in another part of the country, it's a good idea to let them know when you'll be in their region. Of course there's always the chance that they might fly you out for an interview, but don't bank on it.

Basic Closing

I would welcome the opportunity to meet with you to share more about my qualifications, and how I might be able to contribute to the success of Nike.

Thank you for your consideration.

Assertive Closing

I am eager to use my skills and talents to help Hilton maintain its #1 ranking in the hotel industry. I will contact you by phone the week of June 1st to try to arrange an appointment.

Thank you very much for taking the time to review my qualifications.

Closing For the Out-of-Town Job Seeker

I plan to be in Chicago from June 1st through the 15th. If you are interested, and your schedule permits, perhaps we can arrange an appointment for some time during this period. I will call you next Tuesday to discuss this possibility.

Now take a look at a couple examples that incorporate the advice we've outlined so far.

ROB ABLE   444 4th Avenue, 4th floor • Brooklyn, NY • (777) 888-8888

June 1st, 1995

Ms. Jackson
Director of Admissions
University of Georgia
Cheery Lane
Athens, GA 00000

Dear Ms. Jackson:

I am applying for the position of Admissions Representative which you advertised in the May 22nd issue of the *Chronicle of Higher Education*. I recently received my M.A. in Higher Education Administration from Columbia University and have three years of work experience in higher education, two of which have been in admissions.

One theme has remained constant throughout my academic and professional experience: I have excelled at helping others to make sound educational and career decisions. As an Admissions Representative at Bowdoin College I enthusiastically and energetically recruited prospective students, making sure to always listen carefully to their goals and concerns, and respond thoroughly to their questions about college in general and Bowdoin in particular. As a Recruitment Assistant at New York University, in addition to contributing to the organization of a recruitment program featuring over 200 organizations, I frequently assisted students and alumni in formulating and implementing their job search strategies. And finally, as a Human Resources Intern at Met Life, I designed and directed a pre-professional program for minority high school students interested in actuarial science careers. I worked extremely closely with the students, providing them with counseling, advisement, and encouragement.

I would welcome the opportunity to meet with you personally to share more about my background and qualifications, and how I might be able to contribute to the Admissions Department at the University of Georgia. In the meantime, if you have any questions, don't hesitate to call me at (777) 888-8888.

Thank you for your consideration.

Sincerely,

Rob Able

I.M. BIG   000 Bleecker Street, Apt. 29 • New York, NY 10000 • 212-333-3333

May 18, 1995

Thai Dude
The Independent Film Project, Inc.
Carmine Street, #88
New York, NY 11111

Dear Mr. Dude:

I heard about the Communications Specialist opening at your organization through Professor Federico
Allenstonelee of NYU's Tisch School of the Arts. As Professor Allenstonelee described it, the position
requirements and my qualifications seem to match up perfectly.

A year ago I finished my B.A. in Communications at City State University, with a minor in Film.
Since then I have worked in the Public Relations Department of Mirromini Films, where I write press
releases, maintain close ties with the media, and assist with coordinating special events. Previously,
I acquired substantial direct marketing and grant writing experience while interning at the Stone's
Throw, a non-profit organization devoted to the preservation of old rocks. In fact, two of my grant
proposals requesting $20,000 each were funded in full by the city of Bedrock.

As independent film is one of my great passions in life, I would welcome the chance to use my skills
to contribute to the success of your project. I hope to have the opportunity to meet with you in person
to share more about my background and qualifications.

Thank you for your consideration.

Sincerely,

I.M. Big

GETTING YOUR RESUME INTO THEIR HANDS

Should You, or Shouldn't You?

"The best way to send your resume depends to a large extent on an employer's comfort level with technology. Those who embrace new technology would probably be delighted if you send your resume via the Internet, or by fax. Those who are less receptive to new technology would prefer you to mail it."

— Pamela Davies, Recruitment Coordinator, New York University Office of Career Services

The only thing left to do is make sure your letter and resume reach your prospective employer in a timely fashion. There are several ways to accompish this—via mail, fax, courier, and hand delivery. The method you select should really be contingent on A) how badly you want the job, B) how long the job was posted before you heard about it, C) how much of a rush the employer is in to fill the job, and D) the personality type of the prospective employer.

If the position was advertised, the ad usually states the preferred method of resume submission. Follow their directions. In most cases they will ask that you reply by mail, which means it's time for Envelope Stuffing 101. Assuming you're using a standard business envelope, you would first place your cover letter on top of your resume, then fold the documents into thirds so that the blank sides of the paper are showing on both the top and bottom. Then you stuff the package into the envelope and voila, you have your first complete self-marketing package. Just make sure that the letter you place inside the envelope is indeed intended for the addressee. Mix-ups have been known to occur, and it's never a pretty sight when Ms. Johnson opens your package only to find in it a letter that was intended for Mr. Novak.

WHEN YOU NEED SPEED

If time is truly of the essence, the good old U.S. Postal Service may just be a little too slow. Many employers wanted to fill their vacancies yesterday. For the ultimate in speed, faxing is the way to go. First, call the organization and find out if they will accept a fax. If so, terrific, but always supplement your fax by sending a hard copy through the mail. If the organization won't accept a fax or doesn't have a fax machine, you always have the option of sending your package via Federal Express or some other courier service. True, this is an expensive proposition, but in addition to sending your resume, you will be sending a message loud and clear that you want the job pretty badly. In addition to using a courier service, you also have the option of hand delivering your letter and resume, provided the employer is within close proximity. This approach has the added benefit of enabling you to get a peek at your potential place of employment, as well as the opportunity to take a gander at some of your prospective colleagues in action.

FOLLOW-UP IS KEY

You're probably feeling pretty good right now. We'll bet you just sent off ten or so letters and resumes, and now you're thinking it's time to sit back, relax, and wait for the phone to ring. Wrong! It's time to start compiling a list of when you're going to make your follow-up calls. As a general rule give the employer between ten days and two weeks to respond to a written communication. If you've still heard nothing by then, get on the phone and find out if they received your package. If so, ask if they had an opportunity to review your qualifications. Do your best to arrange an interview while you're on the phone with the employer. At the very least, find out when he expects to begin the interviewing process. While you're waiting to hear, you can always drop them a line to reaffirm your interest, and notify him of any recent developments which might enhance your candidacy. This will keep your name fresh in the employer's head and demonstrate that your interest in the job is serious.

Those who don't follow up fall prey to the "out of sight, out of mind" syndrome. Of course you must always be careful not to cross the line between being assertive and being a pain in the butt. If you phone too frequently, you'll be labeled a nuisance. Use your best judgment, and always follow the employer's lead. If she seems visibly perturbed that you're calling her, politely excuse yourself by saying that you just wanted to check on the status of your application, and that you're sorry if you caused her any inconvenience.

CHAPTER 10

THE HI-TECH RESUME

HERE TO STAY OR GONE TOMORROW?

So you think you've got the hang of writing a resume? Now that you've learned all the tricks of the trade, we're going to throw you a curve ball. Recent trends indicate that many large organizations are switching over to computer-based applicant tracking systems to screen resumes. The fact is that computers are much faster and more efficient at reviewing resumes than their human counterparts. Computers can evaluate thousands of resumes in the blink of an eye, and select those that meet the criteria the employer has specified.

COMPUTER ILLITERACY

So what does this all mean for you? Not a whole helluva lot if you're looking for work with a small organization, or if you're hoping to make it in non-traditional fields such as the fine and performing arts. However, if your goal is to climb the corporate ladder at

---

The Best Is Yet to Come

Steve Miller, Manager of Computer and Information Services at the College Placement Council, points out that "it's very difficult to track the results of resume banks and databases. It's extremely hard to get data on placement rates. Part of this may be that usage of these services is still fairly new." Miller suggested that resume databases will probably become more effective once employers are comfortable enough with the technology required to utilize them effectively.

a Fortune 500 company, the implications of the computer resume revolution are substantial. You see, computers don't read the same way people do. They don't have the capacity to make assumptions, interpretations, or read between the lines. Computers can only search for information in a very literal sense. If your resume has the qualifications they've been told to seek by the employer, you're still in the hunt. If not, you're out.

BE NICE TO THE SCANNER

The first hurdle your resume has to face is the scanner. The scanner is an electronic device which translates your resume into a code that the computer can read. Peter Weddle, chairman and CEO of Job Bank USA, offers the following formula to make your resume scanner-friendly.

1. Always laser print your resume.
2. Make sure it arrives flat—use a 9 x 12 inch envelope.
3. Use point sizes no smaller than ten and no larger than fourteen.
4. Don't use italics or graphics.
5. Reserve bold print for headings only.
6. Use fonts without serifs, such as Helvetica or Avant Garde, or with limited serifs, such as Roman.

Unfortunately, even if you adhere to these guidelines there's no guarantee that your resume won't be eaten, mutilated, or permanently lost in cyberland. You might as well put a second resume in the mail just to play it safe.

WORDS ARE KEY

Once you've gotten past the scanner, you'll need to impress the computer. To do this, Mr. Weddle recommends that you include on your resume the keywords that an employer is likely to use in a search. This means thoroughly researching your industry before you submit your resume, and knowing precisely what skills are in demand. Assuming you have these skills, and assuming you include the correct keywords, the chances of your resume being selected for closer scrutiny are pretty high. Of course, at this point you're back to dealing with humans. Hopefully you still remember how to do that.

Resume Databases

Another development that has the potential to significantly alter the way you look for a job is the renaissance of so-called third-party or independent resume database services. These firms have actually been around since the 1960s, but because of recent technological advances they are just now beginning to have a more profound impact on the employment scene.

For a nominal fee, these services offer you the opportunity to have your resume stored on a database which in turn is marketed to employers. The advantage, it would seem, to both employers and job hunters is a tremendous savings in time and money. Employers can gain practically instant access to the resumes of only the most qualified applicants for a mere fraction of what it would cost them to have an employment agency or headhunter do a comparable search. The job hunter, on the other hand, can receive tremendous exposure without the time-consuming and expensive practice of sending out hundreds of resumes.

But Do They Work?

In practice, the effectiveness of resume database services, particularly for college students and recent graduates, has yet to be determined. Very little data is available on placement rates. Also, the general consensus is that these services lend themselves more readily to job hunters who are seeking positions in more conventional fields. If your goal is to find a position in the arts or human services, don't expect a resume database service to be your savior.

Despite their limitations, resume database services certainly can't hurt your job search, and in many cases they may help. The cost of subscription is usually so inexpensive that you might as well give one a try.

A Sampling of Electronic Resume Database Services

cors is the largest recruitment research firm in the country, boasting a database of 1,500,000 professionals. For $25, an individual can have his or her employment profile entered permanently in the database, which is used by a wide variety of employers. According to David Geron, client services marketing manager at cors, companies searching the database for recent graduates are generally looking to fill sales positions, and typically are seeking professionals with backgrounds in marketing and communications. For more information about cors, call 1-800-323-1352.

For a $75 annual fee, **Job Bank USA** provides what chairman and CEO Peter Weddle calls "electronic networking and career insurance" twenty-four hours a day, seven days a week. Approximately fifteen to twenty percent of the 30,000 or so Job Bank USA subscribers are recent graduates, and Weddle's organization has contracts with about seventy alumni associations. Weddle notes that although the single measure of merit of a database service has always been "did you get me a job?," Job Bank USA offers more than just potential placement. Membership includes a quarterly newsletter concerning career management and job search counseling. Job Bank USA can be reached at 1-800-296-1USA.

PEOPLE STILL HIRE PEOPLE

Of course only time will tell whether computerized applicant tracking systems and electronic job hunting become the norm rather than the exception. For now, you need to be aware of the implications of these developments and adjust your approach when necessary. In some cases, you may need to prepare two resumes— one that will satisfy a computer, and one that will satisfy a person.

In the meantime, try not to lose sight of the fact that even in this age of reliance on technological devices to perform tasks that were previously the domain of humans, it is still people who make the hiring decisions. So in the end, the best path to success is to get out there and do some good old-fashioned job hunting.

CHAPTER 11

JOB HUNTING 101

Looking for a career-oriented job is one of the most difficult challenges you'll ever have to face in life. Job hunting requires tremendous physical, mental, and emotional fortitude. It also requires a great deal of time and effort, almost as much as you would devote to a full-time job. This can be particularly strenuous if you're already working or attending school full-time. One full-time job is usually enough for most people.

While you're job hunting, you won't have the luxury of plopping down in front of the tube to watch "Seinfeld" or a ball game when you come home exhausted from work or the classroom. Instead, you'll need to be at your desk writing cover letters, revising your resume, or browsing through the want ads. You'll have to use your vacation time to go on interviews instead of trips. You'll have to use your lunch hour to follow up on job leads. You'll need to be in job hunt mode virtually twenty-four hours a day, seven days a week.

Given the demands of the job hunt, look at yourself in the mirror before you commit to taking the big plunge. Ask yourself if you are really ready to deal with all the hard work, anxiety, pressure, and rejection that a search entails. Be honest. If you're feeling too sensitive, fragile, or insecure, you're better off delaying your search until you're in a better frame of mind. The truth is that a job hunt can have devastating effects on one's self-esteem and confidence. Even the job hunter who's feeling extremely positive and confident at the outset of a search can be quickly worn down after hearing one employer after another say, "we're not interested," "you're not qualified," "you're over-qualified," "we're not hiring at this time," and "we'll keep your resume on file." If at any point in your job hunt you start to feel burnt out, take a break and give yourself a chance to recharge your batteries. Only after you feel reenergized should you gradually ease yourself back into the hunt.

GET CONNECTED

Networking is the most effective job–hunting method known to humankind. Networking means building relationships with professionals in your target field who can provide you with ideas, information, or introductions that will benefit your job search. The adage "it's who you know, not what you know" still holds true. A still more accurate statement would be "it's who you know *and* what you know." One cannot overestimate the power of networking. In a recent survey conducted at a major university, the data revealed that thirty-six percent of the graduates received their first job offer as a result of personal contacts, compared with fourteen percent through on-campus recruitment, and eleven percent through advertisements. The numbers speak for themselves. Besides which, most people find that as they get older, contacts become even more important.

> ### Don't Give Up on Those Want Ads
>
> While networking may be the most effective method of job hunting, responding to advertisements in the newspaper can yield positive results as well. Paula Lee, senior career counselor at New York University, is living proof. Paula got not one, not two, but all three of her professional positions by responding to ads in the *New York Times*.

The point is to put yourself out there, be active, get involved, go to parties, talk to everyone you know. There's no telling who that person is sitting next to you on the bus. He might be your future employer. He might be psychotic. He might be both. You'll just have to take your chances.

FREE LABOR

Interning and volunteering enable you to network, gain related experience, and acquire new skills all at the same time. The internship serves as a trial run where both you and your employer can check each other out to see if the fit is right. Seeking out the right employer is a lot like looking for the right mate. You don't know if it's going to last until you've spent a lot of time together, and you may have to kiss a few frogs before you find a prince (or princess).

> ### The Casting Couch
>
> *"It's not who you know, it's who you do."*
>
> — vice president of a major fragrance company

The good news is that interns are often offered full-time professional positions after concluding their internship. In the same survey cited above, researchers found that about one in ten graduates secured job offers from organizations where they had interned. This trend is not at all surprising considering that employers in the 90s are extremely conscious about hiring costs. Promoting an intern into a full-time position eliminates the need for advertising the job in the newspaper and retaining an employment agency, both of which cost big bucks. It also eliminates the costs of training a brand new employee

C.R.A.P.O.L.A.

We hope we haven't given you the impression that the job hunt is hopeless. We just want you to be prepared for what might happen. Who knows? You may find your ideal job in less than a week, although the average search usually takes closer to six months. There are a staggering number of variables that will affect the outcome of your job hunt. Obviously, if you're well qualified and are seeking a position in a field where the demand for workers exceeds the supply, you should have no problem finding a suitable position.

> **Tough Times Ahead**
>
> The U.S. Department of Education projects that in the year 2005, 1.32 million bachelor's degree holders will be vying for only 914,000 jobs that require post-secondary education, leaving 400,000 graduates to settle for positions that require a high school diploma or less.

Keep in mind, however, that market conditions can fluctuate like your average romance. Just ask the folks who worked on Wall Street in 1989. One day they were sitting on top of the world, and the next day the rug was pulled out from under them. You just can't afford to be complacent in this world. Fortunately, though, there is much you can do to ensure that your job hunt is successful. What you really need is a lot of C.R.A.P.O.L.A.

Creativity

Resourcefulness

Attitude

Persistence

Organization

Luck

Assertiveness

Let's take a closer at these seven virtues.

CREATIVITY

In a tight market flooded with talented job seekers, you need to inject a little creativity into your job hunt. Stay open to new possibilities and approaches. If there is a job that you desperately want, think of every possible angle that might put you in a position to be hired. Resist the temptation to use the same techniques and tactics just because they're familiar. Wear your resume on a T-shirt, have it delivered to your prospective boss with cappuccino and doughnuts, send out press releases, design an innovative business card, put a clever message on your answering machine—the possibilities are endless. Whatever you do, always maintain your professionalism, and try to get noticed in a positive way. Delivering a strip-o-gram to your future company will certainly get you noticed, but you won't be taken seriously.

RESOURCEFULNESS

Being resourceful means leaving no stone unturned. Take advantage of everything and everybody that can be of help in your job search: college career centers, libraries, government agencies, employment agencies, newspapers, magazines, career guides, directories, employer databases, trade associations and publications, and especially people, people, and more people. Since you never know where you might get a tip about a job, you must keep your eyes and ears open at all times. You might be casually flipping through the Sunday paper when bam!, you spot an article about Disney's plans to open a theme park in your hometown. What does that mean? You guessed it—jobs, and lots of them—in marketing, construction, graphic design, management, etc.

Or perhaps you're ambling down main street when you notice that the ground has just been broken for a new hotel and convention center. More jobs. Or maybe you sit down to have lunch with an alum who reveals to you that her friend's record label is looking for an A & R person. Another job. By being resourceful, you'll hear about more opportunities than most of your competitors *combined*. And the more opportunities you hear about, the better the chance you'll come across the one that is just right for you.

Helpful Job Hunting Resources

Job Hunter's Sourcebook, Gale Research—pulls together all of the job hunting resources for 155 high-profile professions.

The Career Guide, Dun & Bradstreet—up-to-date, comprehensive and accurate coverage on prospective employers and career opportunities for recent college graduates.

Encyclopedia of Associations, Gale Research—a guide to 23,000 national and international organizations, including trade, environmental, governmental, educational, technological, health, ethnic, sports, chambers of commerce, and trade and tourism.

Directories in Print, Gale Research—describes more than 14,000 rosters, guides, directory databases, and other lists published in the United States and worldwide. Covers arts and entertainment, business, computers, education, government, health, law, real estate, recreation, science, social services, and other areas.

The National Jobline Directory, Bob Adams—Over 2,000 companies, government agencies and other organizations that post job openings by telephone.

ATTITUDE

A lot of people in this world have an attitude. Hire me because I deserve it. Hire me because I need a job. Hire me because my Dad says you should. Hire me because I'm pretty, tall, white, black, poor, rich, and so on. Wrong attitude! Let's get one thing straight. No employer owes you anything. If you want a job, you have to prove that you deserve it. You have to demonstrate you're the best qualified person, period. That means not only having the necessary talent to perform the work, but also being able to get along well with others. A boss won't care how talented you are if you're a jerk.

Having the right attitude can make all the difference in how an employer perceives you, and could be the one intangible that gets you the nod over the competition. Strive for the three Ps: polite, professional, and, positive. Nobody will hire you if you're rude. Nobody will hire you if you're un-professional. And nobody will hire you if you're a downer. This applies not only to how you behave on your interviews but to how you conduct yourself at all times during the job hunt. Treat the people in the mailroom and at the reception desk with the same courtesy and respect that you would show a top executive. Never criticize former employers or colleagues, and don't make excuses for your shortcomings.

Project as much enthusiasm, energy, and pep as possible. Show the employer that you're a dynamo. Let her know that you're ready for long hours, working weekends, and whatever else it takes to get the job done. Make the case that you're a team player and that you're willing to make sacrifices for the good of the organization.

PERSISTENCE

"Don't give up, don't ever give up." Those are the words of the late Jim Valvano, former basketball coach of the North Carolina State Wolfpack, who in 1981 led a team of overachievers to the NCAA title. Coach V. would not have too much regard for slackers, and neither do employers.

Valvano's legacy is a meaningful one for the job hunter. If you work hard, and believe in yourself, eventually good things will happen. Stay on course and be patient. When you feel like quitting just remind yourself how far you've come and that success could be just around the corner. Stay focused, determined, and keep hammering away. Yes, there will be rejection, and yes, there will be frustration, but if you're persistent the fruits of your labor will flourish.

ORGANIZATION

To job hunt successfully you must maintain extremely accurate records, and be able to competently manage mountains of information. You have to keep track of what you sent to whom and when. Be organized. Approaching your job hunt in an organized manner will prevent such mistakes from happening. And by organized, I don't mean sticking Post-Its all over your mirror. I mean buying a notebook or looseleaf and keeping track of all the information and activities that pertain to your job hunt. For each target employer this might include: a profile of the organization and a description of the job that's available; copies of all the job search communications you've sent; a list of the phone calls you made to the organization and the outcomes of those calls; dates for follow-up by phone or mail; your impressions of the interview; and the pros and cons of the job offer.

Try to devise a system that works for you. The most elaborate job–hunting log in the world is completely useless if it doesn't suit your style. How you keep track of your search doesn't really matter so long as you do it in a way that you can follow. Maybe Post-Its aren't so bad after all.

LUCK

Yes, you read correctly. Although some would argue that by definition luck is out of your control, we disagree. People often get lucky because they put themselves in a position to be lucky. You win the lottery because you bought the ticket. The half-court hook shot goes in at the buzzer because you made sure you released the ball as soon as you caught it. It's not a pure coincidence that you happen to be in the right place at the right time. How to enhance the luck factor? Take a nice, big, deep breath, round up all those ugly, negative thoughts swimming around your head, and as you exhale blow them all away for ever and ever. Now go play the lottery.

ASSERTIVENESS

Job hunting is no time to be passive or shy. If this is your tendency, you may find yourself being passed over by employers for those who are more outgoing. Unfortunately, being assertive doesn't come naturally to all of us. Many of us have been discouraged from being assertive by parents who consider such behavior rude or inappropriate. Others have been raised in a cultural milieu where assertiveness is not the norm. It may take you a little while to reorient yourself. Try practicing being assertive with friends first until you get the hang of it. You might also consider signing up for an assertiveness training seminar.

Of course we're not saying that you have to change your entire personality, at least not permanently. But for the duration of your job hunt you'll find that pursuing what you want in an assertive manner will make a difference.

For example, if you're attending a career fair or alumni panel discussion, you need to strut right up to the participants and introduce yourself. Give them a copy of your resume and ask for their business card. In contrast, the shrinking violet posture will get you nowhere. It stands to reason that if nobody knows you're out there, then there's no way in the world they'll be able to hire you. It's like going to a party and spending the entire evening doing your best imitation of a wallflower. How many new friends do you think you'll make?

You also need to be an opportunist. If you see an opening, don't hesitate—just go for it! One of our former students was on a bike trip with a few of his buddies the week following graduation. He was lamenting about the prospect of finding a job in the publishing field. Minutes later, the cyclists pulled over for a water stop where an older gentleman was quenching his thirst. It turned out that this gentleman just happened to be the president of a publishing company, and just happened to be in need of an administrative assistant for the summer. Seizing the moment, the student struck up a conversation with the executive, expressed his desire to be in publishing, and landed himself a job. After working the summer as an administrative assistant, he was offered a full-time position in the fall as an editorial assistant.

Now keep in mind that there is a definite distinction between being assertive and being aggressive. Being assertive is moving forward in a confident and positive manner. Being aggressive is using a forceful and combative approach which often infringes on the rights of the person you're approaching. Try not to forget this distinction.

Go Get 'Em

Well what are you waiting for? Go out there with your head way up high and give them lots of C.R.A.P.O.L.A. We wish you the best of luck.

ABOUT THE AUTHOR

Since 1988 Tim Haft has counseled thousands of college students and alumni on all aspects of the career planning process. Since completing his M.A. in Sociology at New York University and his B.A. in History at the University of Virginia, he has worked as a career counselor at New York University, the Fashion Institute of Technology, and the City University of New York. Haft is also the founder of Trashproof Resumes, a New York-based resume consulting firm, and is a member of Creative Pursuits, a multidisciplinary team of clinicians providing psychotherapy and career counseling to the artistic community.

NOTES

NOTES

NOTES